FAMOUS REGIMENTS

The Life Guards

Other titles in this series
The Royal Horse Guards [The Blues]
The 10th Royal Hussars
The 11th Hussars
The 17th/21st Lancers
The Royal Tank Regiment
The Scots Guards
The Queen's Royal Regiment (West Surrey)
The Royal Northumberland Fusiliers
The Royal Fusiliers
The Royal Norfolk Regiment
The Suffolk Regiment
The Somerset Light Infantry
The East Yorkshire Regiment
The Bedfordshire and Hertfordshire Regiment
The Green Howards
The Lancashire Fusiliers
The South Wales Borderers
The Worcestershire Regiment
The Duke of Cornwall's Light Infantry
The Duke of Wellington's Regiment (West Riding)
The Royal Hampshire Regiment
The Black Watch
The Oxfordshire and Buckinghamshire Light Infantry
The Royal Berkshire Regiment
The King's Own Yorkshire Light Infantry
The King's Royal Rifle Corps
The Wiltshire Regiment
The North Staffordshire Regiment
The York and Lancaster Regiment
The Highland Light Infantry
The Gordon Highlanders
The Argyll and Sutherland Highlanders
The Rhodesian African Rifles
The Royal Army Service Corps
The Royal Flying Corps

FAMOUS REGIMENTS

Edited by
Lt.-General Sir Brian Horrocks

The Life Guards

by R. J. T. Hills

Leo Cooper Ltd., London

First published in Great Britain, 1971
by Leo Cooper Ltd.,
196 *Shaftesbury Avenue, London W.C.*2

ISBN 0 85052 087 8

Printed in Great Britain by
Compton Press, Compton Chamberlayne, Salisbury, Wilts.

The Life Guards

INTRODUCTION

by Lt.-General Sir Brian Horrocks

COLONEL HILLS has spent thirty years in The Life Guards and this book is clearly a labour of love. Although he pulls no punches, every paragraph is imbued with the deep affection and admiration he feels for his regiment. As a result he has produced a fascinating account of a comparatively little-known aspect of British history. For his regiment is unique in the military world, its chief function having always been the protection of the Sovereign.

The Life Guards trace their formation back to the two troops of royalist gentlemen who followed Charles II into exile in 1651. An officer of the Life Guards always attended upon the King, 'from his rising to his going to bed', and his badge of office was, and still is, an ebony staff with a gold head. Ready to relieve 'Gold Stick', as he was called, was another officer called 'Silver Stick'. Full Colonels of the two Household Cavalry Regiments still do duty as 'Gold Stick' —the nearest military officer to the sovereign. 'Silver Stick' is now the officer commanding the Household Cavalry.

In those early days it was essential for the Sovereign to have a close personal guard on duty in the royal palace and the practice, while no longer a matter of security, survives on state occasions to the present day. In 1949 I was appointed Gentleman Usher of the Black Rod, the Sovereign's representative in the House of Lords, and it was my privilege to stand with the Earl Marshal and the Lord Chancellor at the Sovereign's entrance, prior to the State Opening of Parliament. The Royal Coach, with its escort of Household Cavalry, would come clattering down the embankment. Both sides of the stairs leading from the Royal Entrance to the Robing Room were already lined by dismounted troopers from the Household Cavalry. The procession would pass up the stairs through the ranks of the only serving soldiers with the right and privilege to be on duty in a royal palace.

The Household Cavalry, which until 1922 consisted of the Royal Horse Guards and the two regiments of The Life Guards, is perhaps the most exclusive and expensive military 'club' in the world. The social life of the Court, in which the Household Cavalry were expected to participate, was always financially demanding—thus restricting recruits into the commissioned ranks of the Household Cavalry to a small *élite* of very rich young men to whom their army pay, as one officer remarked, was 'a mockery'. The fact that none of the officers was dependent upon the army for their livelihood gave them an independant outlook and a readiness to rely upon their own initiative which has contribute enormously to their success on the battlefield.

The regiment has always attracted a very high standard of long-service enlisted men to whom a considerable degree of authority could be delegated and I cannot end this introduction better than by mentioning Corporal of Horse Thompson who won a D.C.M. for his gallantry in Belgium in 1944, won the King's Cup at Olympia, was second in the Prince of Wales' Cup in 1949, and was 1st, 2nd and 3rd in the King's Cup and 1st and 2nd in The Prince of Wales's Cup in 1950. In 1951 he was commissioned Riding Master, the only one in the British Army.

Since the end of the last war, British troops have been continuously engaged in peace-keeping rôles throughout the world and, armoured cars being particularly suitable for this type of work, the Life Guards have seen service in Palestine, Cyprus, Malaysia, Hong Kong, Germany, Aden and Northern Ireland. Colonel Hills quotes a warrant officer who remarked, 'We're a peaceful crowd really, but if we have to fight—well, we just do our best'. As a Corps Commander who was always delighted to have them under his command, I know how good, how very good indeed, that best is.

Acknowledgements

THE whole inspiration for this book is over thirty years' service in the Regiment, whose members, of all ranks, could never have given truer comradeship. To them my deepest gratitude is due.

Of written works, I have based my narrative on *The Story of the Household Cavalry* by the late Sir George Arthur, Bt., C.V.O., and the war histories of the two Household Cavalry Regiments by Colonel the Hon. E. H. Wyndham, M.C., and Major Roden Orde. So much that is useful has been dug from the *Household Brigade Magazine* (now the *Guards' Magazine*) and the *Journal of the Society for Army Historical Research.*

Acknowledgement of the sources of pictures has been made in the captions and I am grateful to Messrs. Cassell and Co. Ltd. for permission to publish extracts from the *Journal of Assistant Surgeon James* by Jane Vansittart.

At the London end Mr. L. V. Shaw has again looked after my interests and has been more than helpful in chasing up pictures and their owners.

The Household Cavalry are fortunate in possessing one of the Army's finest museums and the help of its staff, especially that of Squadron Corporal Major C. W. Frearson, has been so readily given that it is almost – but must not be – taken for granted. Lieutenant-Colonel E. S. Nicholls has supplied the personal touch in the later chapters and Colonel Ian B. Baillie, in reading my MS, has guided me round a few perilous corners. For the score of the Regimental March I am indebted to Captain A. J. Jackson, Director of Music.

We are a proud regiment, and believe that we have

reason to be so. Perhaps our character was summed up accurately when a serving warrant officer remarked to the present writer recently: 'We're a pretty peaceful crowd really; but, if we have to fight – well, we just do our best.'

Chapter I

The King Enjoys His Own Again

WHEN this century was young and less sophisticated English schoolboys went to school once a year with sprays of oak leaves in their caps. The day was known as 'Oakapple Day' and there was a jingle to fit the occasion:

'The twentyninth of May
Is the King's Birthday.'

But the birthday had nothing to do with the reigning monarch, nor with any of his direct ancestors.

History was then made up of stories and one of the most popular was that of King Charles II, an uncrowned fugitive, who in 1651 sought refuge from Cromwell's troopers in the Boscobel Oak, from which all the 'Royal Oaks' of Britain are descended. Thus the oak leaves became his symbol, worn on his birthday, the happiest being that of 1660, when he 'came into his own again', riding serenely into his capital and home town of London.

He came 'with a triumph of above 20,000 horse and foot, brandishing their swords and shouting with inexpressible joy; the ways strewed with flowers, the bells ringing, the streets hung with tapisseries, fountains running wine . . . trumpets, music and myriads of people even so far as Rochester.' So wrote old John Evelyn who 'stood in the Strand and beheld it and blessed God.' But no one in the King's entourage could have 'brandished their swords' with more joy than the eighty gentlemen nearest him, for they were his Life Guard, come with him from exile.

It is from that glad day that today's Life Guards, their descendants, date their existence. Oak leaves and acorns flourish on their helmet plates: officers wear gold lace of the same pattern. When, in 1918, regimental signs were ordered for unit transport in France, the First Life Guards chose the historic distinction: while today the regimental magazine is *The Acorn*.

* * *

The Regiment was really born earlier than 1660, for the exiled Charles had a court of loyalists more needy even than he. All they had was their swords – and their duty to their Prince. Charles attracted loyalty. 'May I never drink wine again,' said one soldier of fortune, 'if I had not rather live at six sous a day with him than have all the pleasures of this world without him.' Thus a Guard was raised for him and formed into a troop of eighty private gentlemen. He needed them for his actual protection and also to preserve something of the dignity that must surround even ragged royalty out of office. Much later, when he was really king, Charles once announced to Lord Chancellor Hyde that he must go down to Tonbridge to visit his sister.

'I suppose,' remarked the cautious official, 'you will go with a light train?'

'I intended to take nothing but my night bag.'

'You will not go without forty or fifty horse?' urged the other. The king's wit was ready for the occasion.

'I count that part of my night bag!'

Breda is usually given as the Regiment's birthplace, though it may have been Brussels or even Cologne. Charles, whose later anxiety was never to go on his travels again, changed his lodgings according to the latest policies of his hosts or the credit allowed him by local tradesmen. He once had to run from Holland because Cromwell insisted that the Dutch should arrest him, but he was in Breda when he at last had the call to return; it was in Breda that his Life Guard was organised and from Breda that they brought him home, via the Hague.

In command of the Guard rode Charles, Baron Gerard of Brandon, later Earl of Macclesfield. An out-and-out cavalier from Lancashire, he had brought his own troop to fight for Charles I and commanded a brigade at Edgehill, where he was wounded. A lieutenant-general under Rupert, he went with him abroad when all was lost and saw service in the naval squadron that remained loyal to the monarchy, paying its way with a little buccaneering on the side.

Neither the idea nor the title of 'Life Guard' were new to Britain. The King's father had a Life Guard at least as early as 1641 at the 'Corps de Garde House within the Railes by Whitehall'. Thc Guard rode with him to battle, being known, a little enviously, as 'The Golden Troop'. Charles II, in his bid for the throne in 1650, was escorted by a Scots Troop of Life Guards under the Earl of Newburgh, while even Cromwell had his 'Life Guard of Horse'. George Monck, who became Duke of Albemarle at the Restoration, brought his Life Guard down from Scotland with him, while James, Duke of York left his behind at Dunkirk, where they took over from the troops of the Commonwealth.

Army titles were not rigid then and Charles' men were known indifferently as 'The Life Guard', 'Horse Guard', or 'The Life Guard of Horse'. In their original form the Horse Guards buildings – not quite on the original site, replaced the ruinous 'Corps de Garde' and formed a gateway to Whitehall Palace. The sentries still face inwards today because Whitehall was a public thoroughfare through the precincts and had to be watched. The western side was looked after by mounted patrols and by Foot Guard sentries from the Tilt Yard Guard on the present Horse Guards Parade. Passage through the Guard in wheeled vehicles is still restricted to a very few officials 'having Her Majesty's permission to do so'. They are issued with an ivory pass for the purpose.

* * *

This picture, by John Wyck, c. 1672, is probably the earliest representation of a British cavalry regimental uniform. The subject is Major-General Randolph, but his uniform is that of a lieutenant of Life Guards, which appointment he held on the original establishment of 1660.

By kind permission of Brigadier T. F. J. Collins

Economy soon dealt ponderous blows at the 'twenty thousand horse and foot' – to say nothing of the sullen remnants of Cromwell's men who had lined the King's way at Blackheath. The army, symbolic of newly-escaped tyranny, was ordered to be disbanded, except that the King was left free to retain as a bodyguard 'such as His Majesty shall think fit to dispose of and maintain at his own expense'. Thus it is that the Life Guards can claim descent from the eighty men of Breda. In the general flood of disbandments the Duke of Albemarle's troop of Life Guards, together with his regiment of foot – today the Coldstream Guards – were given the privilege of being left until last, while the

Duke of York kept his own troop in being at Dunkirk, where they could remain under the double heading of 'Guards and Garrisons'.

Thus matters stood when, early in 1661, the Venner riots broke out in London. Venner's supporters were republican fanatics, but any excuse was good enough for the London mob: murder and looting were let loose. The King was out of town, but the Coldstreamers and what was left of the Life Guard reacted strongly. While the Coldstream skirmished out at Hampstead, the Life Guards rode down into the City and ran the hard core of the rebels to earth in a Wood Street alehouse. A handyman from the Navy, one Lambert, climbed along the tiles and broke in upon the rebels from above.

King Charles had the grounds he needed. His own troop of Life Guards stood intact: he brought his brother's home from France: saved Albemarle's to become the Third Troop: while up in Scotland the Scot's Troop was re-raised under its original commander, the Earl of Newburgh. Gerard of Brandon retained his troop, with overall command of the whole body, living in the Cockpit, roughly where Downing Street runs today. It is possible that the ceremony of Trooping the Colour, or at any rate the siting of it, originated in the daily bringing out on parade of the Standard from the colonel's quarters where it would normally be lodged.

The King's Troop mustered, besides its captain, four lieutenants, a cornet, a quartermaster, four brigadiers, a chaplain and a surgeon. It had four trumpeters, a kettle-drummer and 200 private gentlemen, the remaining troops being slightly weaker. Each man had his sword, two pistols and a carbine. Low-crowned, broad-brimmed hats with plumes gave the gay touch, but they had pistol-proof linings. Scarlet coats were gold laced: sashes and gauntlets, cloaks and capes, with leather breeches and jacked boots completed the picture, while buff jackets and cuirasses were issued for service. The different troops could be distinguished by the colours of their ribbons and horse furniture.

The establishment was filled from the ample reservoir of loyal gentlemen out of employ, many of them ruined in the royal service and bearing high rank in the army. Thus, in the King's Troop, of the four original lieutenants the senior was Major-General Egerton and another a colonel. The quartermaster and all four brigadiers were also colonels. There were no non-commissioned officers, 'right-hand men' being nominated for drill purposes.

Pluralism was rife within the new army as in public life, but it would be hard to better the record of Lieutenant Thomas Panton. In addition to his post in the Life Guards he had a company in the Foot Guards and was a paymaster in the Fleet. On the private side he was the owner of Piccadilly Hall, a prosperous gaming establishment. One night, having fairly cleared the board, he vowed never to play again and turned building speculator instead. He left Panton Street in London's West End to perpetuate his name and work.

The grossly exaggerated revelations of the 'Popish Plot' of 1678 did not worry the easy-going Charles unduly, but the nation took another view of his danger. Captains of troops of Life Guards (all, of course, of high rank) were now, by rota, entrusted with the duty of attending upon the King from 'his rising to his going to bed', coming 'next the King's person before all others'. This guardian's badge of office was (and still is) an ebony staff with a golden head, the first issue being paid for on January 7, 1679. Ready to relieve Gold Stick on occasion came Silverstick, also a Life Guard officer. Full colonels of the two Household Cavalry regiments still do duty as Gold Stick, the nearest military officer to the Sovereign. Silverstick is the Officer Commanding Household Cavalry.

Lifeguardsmen were responsible for the King's safety

everywhere 'except within the royal bedchamber' where the Yeomen of the Guard took over. The right of the Life Guards – and with them today the Blues and Royals – to do duty within the royal palaces is emphasized by the 'Staircase Party' which attends the House of Lords (i.e. the 'Palace of Westminster') for State Openings of Parliament. Troopers still do duty outside the ballroom of Buckingham Palace, a duty they first performed at Whitehall in 1664. They provided their first escort for an opening of Parliament in 1671.

* * *

The honeymoon period between king and nation was climaxed by the coronation on St. George's Day, 1661. The royal procession from the Tower to Westminster was headed by the Duke of York's Troop with their trumpets and kettledrums. The King's Troop followed the monarch himself, with that of the Duke of Albemarle bringing up the rear. General duties were pleasant and not often strenuous. London was their playground, Horse Guards their club.

'To Whitehall to the Gatehouse,' wrote a gentleman in 1662. 'I was had into the Guardroom, which I thought to be Hell: some therein were sleeping, other swearing, others smoking tobacco. In the chimney of the room I believe there were two bushels of broken tobacco pipes, almost half a load of ashes.'

Tobacco growing was, incidentally, a monopoly of the colony of Virginia which, with smoking rapidly becoming a vice, had to be protected. On one occasion a detachment of Life Guards was sent down to Winchcombe in Gloucestershire to burn an illegal crop of the weed.

The normal Whitehall guard was 100-strong and was available to deal with trouble anywhere in London. When the Court travelled – and Charles was highly mobile – the complement was 180 private gentlemen. In the absence of barracks, billeting was a problem. At Windsor, for instance, men and horses were distributed between the 'inns, victualling houses, taverns, brandy houses and ale houses' as far afield as Egham, Staines, Oakingham and Chertsey, with an inlying picquet in the 'next one or two inns to our Castle of Windsor'. Up to very recent times two corporals of horse on court duty in the Castle were billeted regularly either in the 'White Hart' or the 'Castle Hotel'.

The country was practically without police and the civil authorities could only look to the military to preserve order. Restoration London took even its fun and games seriously, and a free-for-all was welcome. There was one such when, in 1661, the ambassadors of France, Spain and Sweden disembarked together at Tower Wharf. The Swedes got away in good order but France and Spain fought it out for second place. The Duke of York had sent his troop to see fair play and they formed a ring for the contestants, from the circumference of which delighted Cockneys hurled impartial bricks. The Spaniards hamstrung two of the French horses and won the race with half-an-hour to spare, the Frenchman finishing the course on two wheels.

Lifeguardsmen were typical of their times and, quartered about the town when not on duty, difficult to discipline. Later in the reign they paid entrance money to get into the corps and could sell out when dissatisfied. Duels were frequent, there were riots and drunken quarrels. The obvious remedy was the building of barracks – of which the civil establishment was highly suspicious – but orders were duly given for the provision of stabling, at least, in Leicester Fields and Hyde Park, the latter being the origin of Knightsbridge Barracks.

Charles worked swiftly in the raising of a royal army, the lack of which had been the cause of his father's downfall. By mid-1662 he could review in Hyde Park the 'Guards – being of Horse and Foot 4,000, led by General the Duke of Albemarle . . . consisting of gentlemen of quality and veteran soldiers'. A most important step was taken when, in 1678, detachments of Horse Grenadiers were raised to accompany the troops of Life Guards. Finally established in 1684, a troop was attached to each troop of Life Guards. These men were, in contrast to the Life Guards proper, enlisted soldiers who were regimented in 1693. Their headquarters were the Royal Mews at Charing Cross, where the National Gallery now stands.

Grenadiers, both horse and foot, were a fashionable development, though the mounted variety soon ceased to operate in their nominal role. The Horse Grenadiers (soon adding 'Guards' to their title), provided advanced and rear guards to escorts and normally accompanied the King when he went out on foot. This could be strenuous enough in the company of this athletic monarch. His morning walk across the park and up Constitution Hill kept them fit enough.

'The King,' commented Evelyn, 'now augmented his Guards with a new sort of dragoons who carried granadoes and were habitted after the Polish manner, with long peaked caps, very fierce and fantastical.' Each troop was established at a strength of two lieutenants, two sergeants, two corporals, four hautboys, two drummers and 64 grenadiers. Their nominal mounted infantry function is emphasized by their having sergeants instead of corporals of horse, and no kettledrums or trumpets.

Whatever the incidental duties of the Life Guards about London, the real effect of their existence can be seen in an attack on the establishment made in Parliament when they were denounced as a standing army in disguise. Lord Shaftesbury, generally at the bottom of any plotting, remarked at the time: 'Little good is to be had from the King as long as he has his guards about him: if it were not for them we would quickly go down to Whitehall and obtain what terms we thought fit.' But Charles had learned the lesson of his father's death.

Gerard of Brandon lost his post in 1668. He was a difficult person to deal with and, after the fashion of his times, lax in money matters. There was no personal accusation against him but his clerk, William Carr, tried to make a dash for France with fifteen hundred pounds of public money. Gerard, with adequate financial persuasion, made way for the Duke of Monmouth, the King's eldest natural son. It was in the same year that the indefatigable Samuel Pepys, 'took a hackney coach' to Hyde Park to watch a royal review, which he found 'mighty fine and the Duke of Monmouth in mighty rich clothes'.

There was a crisis at court when, in 1670, the Duke of Albemarle died and his troop became the Queen's. This entailed it being stepped up into second place over that of the Duke of York, always very much on his dignity. He protested strongly, but Charles had his way, as he usually managed to do over much more important matters.

There was yet another function performed by the Life Guards. They became an elementary form of officers' training corps. A writer of 1679 describes them as 'six hundred young men of very considerable families who are there made fit for military service'. Charles was building an army and was determined that it should be a royal one. These picturesque young gentlemen were his future officers.

Chapter 2

Alarums & Excursions

ROISTERING around London or clattering out to Newmarket or Windsor with their master was by no means sufficient outlet for the turbulent spirits of young guardsmen. Their ostensible trade was war and they sought it where it could be found. If the army could not provide it then the Royal Navy might. The deck of a ship could be more restive than the back of a horse, but ships were still normally fought by soldiers, mostly gentlemen volunteers as they had been in Armada days. Prince Rupert was as famous a 'general at sea' as he had been a cavalryman: both the Duke of York and even old Monck took readily to the trade.

Despite the hospitality that he had received from the Netherlands and his close family ties with the House of Orange, the main enemy of King Charles' country was the Dutch Republic under its Stadtholder. Dutch and British were the chief merchants and shipowners of Europe and therefore natural rivals. England was placed ideally for a naval war against Holland. She could snap up home-coming Dutch merchantmen, and the wars of the reign were paying times for British sailors. The line between naval warfare and plain piracy was thin, and the sailors need not wait until heralds had proclaimed war in London.

The First Dutch War was declared on February 22, 1665, and the proclamation was received 'with shouts of joy' at Westminster, Temple Bar and the Royal Exchange, the attendant Life Guards 'drawing their swords and clattering them'. A number of them volunteered for sea service, being allowed to retain their appointments and pay.

Naval operations on a major scale began with an action

off Lowestoft on June 3, the Duke of York and Prince Rupert commanding for Britain, with High Admiral Opdam on the other side, and under them the 'two most mighty and best-appointed Fleets which any age had ever seen'. The guns were heard in London, and when news trickled through it told of a great victory. The Dutch lost twenty ships and 8,000 men, including their admiral – the British no more than 800. But among the killed was the first officer casualty of the Life Guards. Lord Falmouth, commanding officer of the Duke of York's Troop, was killed at the side of his master and friend.

* * *

In the Second Dutch War, which began in 1672, the Life Guards found more orthodox employment. England was now allied with the French, who marched an army into the Low Countries. An English contingent under the Duke of Monmouth included a service troop of Life Guards under the direct command of Louis Duras, a French Huguenot, later to become Earl of Feversham, who had taken over the Duke of York's Troop. One hundred and fifty lifeguardsmen made up the detachment.

The opening campaign was a stately seventeenth-century march to invest the Rhine fortresses, capture Utrecht and establish a blockade round Maastricht. It was ambitious enough for a summer campaign, and turned out to be little more than a reconnaissance. In the inevitable retirement to winter quarters the Life Guards saw Paris for the first time. Next spring, with Monmouth now a lieutenant-general, Louis of France got down to the siege of Maastricht in earnest. Monmouth's own command was considerable – 8,000 men in all. The decisive action came at the end of June, when the Duke was ordered to make a lodgement in the fortifications.

Throughout the night his men dug their way from their

own trenches to the selected point of attack – the 'Green Half Moon,' but, just as they were preparing for the final assault, the enemy sprung a mine beneath their feet. Monmouth reinforced his troops with a detachment of the Black Musketeers, then, followed by twelve volunteers of the Life Guards, he sprang from the trench.

'Through a storm of shot,' runs a contemporary account, 'he marched with all the speed he could to the Half Moon, passing through a sally port of the enemy's and so all among within twenty yards of their Palisadoes, being followed by Monsieur d'Artagnan and the Musketeers.' The attack was decisive, though they had to withstand a counter-attack. Among the killed was d'Artagnan, later more famous as the hero of *The Three Musketeers*. The war petered out and peace was signed in February 1674. Thus, the Life Guards were blooded to continental warfare and marched home via Dieppe, less one third of their number as casualties.

* * *

Five years later the Scots Troop was in action in its own country, where there was a serious rising of Covenanters, who had butchered Archbishop Sharpe of St. Andrews. Monmouth was in command of the forces detailed to suppress the rising. There was a sharp action at Bothwell Brig, where the Scots Troop gained distinction and the rebels were routed.

But the main enemy remained entrenched at Westminster, where the Commons came up with their 'Quest of Grievances' of 1674. They found eight reasons for dismissing the Guards. They were (among other things) illegal, the King having no official protection save the Gentlemen Pensioners and his Yeomen. They were also a 'vast charge' – so much so that if the King had not them to pay he might have settled all his other debts without 'burdening his good people with taxes'. They formed a place of refuge for

The Scots Troop of Life Guards, with Kettledrummer and Trumpeters, at the first opening of Parliament in Edinburgh under James II and VII.

Contemporary engraving by Thos Summers

Papists (a popular cry) and they were 'altogether useless . . . as doth plainly appear by His Majesty's most happy and peaceable reign'.

Happy the King usually contrived to be: 'peaceable' was an over-simplification. His use of the guards was generally discreet but he felt the more secure for their presence. He was successful, with their help, in first removing Parliament to Oxford and then dissolving it. There was continual plotting by religious extremists and there was a decided effort to set up Monmouth – 'the Protestant Duke' – as Charles' legitimate heir. In 1682 Shaftesbury made a last bid for revolution on the anniversary of Queen Elizabeth's accession, which, with Guy Fawkes Day, were the two great London Protestant festivals.

Charles was advised to send the Life Guards down to the City, but objected that he 'did not love to play with his Horse' and left the matter to the sheriffs. The Rye House Plot of a year later was even more serious and might well have succeeded. Based on the fact that Charles in his coach usually out-distanced his escort, he and his brother were to be shot from a ditch on the way from Newmarket to London. Accident outwitted the plotters. The royal house at Newmarket was burned down one night and the King came up to London a day earlier than planned.

King Charles II left his realms reasonably prosperous and contented. He may not have been the pattern of a great monarch, but he founded the British Army and his Life Guards rode down into history. One of the official witnesses to the decease of the monarch was the Earl of Feversham, now commanding the Life Guard.

* * *

When James II came to the throne in 1685 there was little inkling of trouble, for he reaped the benefits of his brother's popularity and astuteness. Men were well aware of his religious views, but were prepared to regard them as his own affair, especially as, in his first address to the Privy Council, he stated his intention to 'preserve the government both in Church and State as it is by law established'. Even when he attended Mass in public, Anglican eyebrows were merely raised. Only later – when he was recognised as an unrelenting bigot – men started to recall tales of 'Bloody Mary' and the fires of Smithfield.

The Monmouth rebellion, though it sounds dramatic, was no more than a ripple on the surface of national life. The West Country peasants who joined Monmouth and suffered for him were notorious for their fanaticism and it was as the 'Protestant Duke' that Monmouth came, though it was only a matter of days before he was signing himself 'James R.' Despite his earlier capability as a soldier, he was the seventeenth-century example of a playboy, courting the dregs of the London population, tool of the unscrupulous, profligate in private life and hesitant in action.

He landed at Lyme Regis on June 11, 1685, heading a sorry collection of fanatics and adventurers, a supporting rebellion in Scotland going off at half-cock. The peasantry who flocked to him were undrilled and lacking in arms, though he had some success in attracting deserters from local militia units.

It was now that John Churchill stepped outside the pages of purely regimental history. He had served in the First Guards and was made Colonel of the Royal Dragoons when they were brought home from Tangier to the home establishment. James' first reaction to the invasion news was to appoint Churchill brigadier and send him off in command of the first troops available – four troops of the Blues, four of the Royals and five companies of the Queen's (the 2nd Foot, known as 'Kirke's Lambs'). Feversham was appointed Commander-in-Chief and ordered to follow up with sufficient men to crush the rebellion before it could spread.

Churchill headed the rebels off from Bristol and contained them until his chief could come up. Feversham was a tidy-minded general and treated the rebels with a respect they had hardly earned. He had most of his own Third Troop of Life Guards with him, plus their Horse Grenadiers, the rest of the Blues and Queen's, the Royal Scots and Trelawney's (4th Foot, King's Own Royal Regiment). As he marched he concentrated until, as one excited lady in London had it: 'All His Majesty's forces are now hemming in Monmouth and he must fight his way through or perish. Our ears are full of drums and trumpets.'

Monmouth blew hot and cold by fits, but it was by no means such an easy task for the Royalists as it might seem, fighting against fanatics with their lives at stake and in abominable weather. The rebels had their small successes, capturing a wagon from the Queen's full of arms and cash. In their enthusiasm they wrecked Wells Cathedral.

A detachment of Life Guards under Major Theophilus Oglethorpe had an exciting preliminary skirmish, until at last the careful Feversham was in position. The battle of Sedgemoor, which followed, settled James – as he thought – on the throne.

Monmouth gave signs of intending to advance and the royal army was disposed along the line of a great ditch known as the Bussex Rhine. It was this ditch which, imperfectly mapped, was to be Monmouth's undoing. The day was Sunday, July 5, and the King's general felt justified in taking it easy. Most of his cavalry took up billets and got busy with the bottle, while he himself went calmly to bed.

Monmouth, his mood changing again, was planning in his despair to escape to Cheshire, when news came that the Royalists were making a drunken night of it. He sent off his few mounted men under Lord Grey to outflank the enemy and catch them in the rear. Oglethorpe failed to detect the move and, before he could correct his mistake and get back to headquarters, the fight had begun.

Drunk or sober the Royalists were more than a match for raw rebels, stumbling in the dark against the unsuspected 'Rhine'. Grey's so-called cavalry fled, leaving the foot to fight it out. Feversham let the ever-alert Churchill fight his own battle, while he directed parties of Life Guards and Blues round both enemy flanks. Churchill had trouble with his guns, but got three of them into action, with the powerful aid of the Bishop of Winchester, who hitched in his own coach horses and even served a gun himself.

Dawn saw the end of the whole wretched business. The Royalists made a general advance over the ditch; Monmouth fled, two of his battalions alone standing for a fight to the end. As the peasants were rounded up Feversham started a course of immediate hanging, until his militant bishop reminded him that there was a law in the land which, personified in Judge Jeffries, did not prove more lenient.

Rewards were handed out. Feversham got the Garter and the First Troop of Life Guards, Churchill, now major-general, taking over the Third Troop with overall command of the Guard. The lion of the hour in London was Oglethorpe who, having brought the news to Court, was knighted and made colonel. Unlike so many of his comrades, he remained loyal to James and refused service under his successor.

James lulled himself into the belief that the mass of the nation was still behind him; he was, however, under no delusion as to the strength of the faction working against him. Above all, he mistrusted William of Orange, his own son-in-law but the true protestant champion; a soldier and member of the royal house. There was constant coming and going between London and the Hague by men who knew well what was at stake.

The King set himself to build up and organise his army. He was a keen soldier and holds the record of having commanded both the French Army and the Royal Navy. He organised a training camp at Hounslow which served to overawe the Cockneys and to warn William. His great mistake was to bring in Irish troops and to admit – against the law – Catholic officers. In May 1686 he raised a Fourth Troop of Life Guards (the Scots Troop had no number) under Lord Dover, himself a Catholic, with orders to enroll none but gentlemen of that religion. But Dover was a man of business, and accepted all comers at forty guineas a head. The Life Guards, including the Horse Grenadiers, now mustered well over a thousand. The British Army, one authority could claim, was now accounted 'the best paid, the best appointed and the best disciplined in Europe' – yet it let its builder down.

The decision to declare the 'Glorious Revolution' was forced by the birth of a Prince of Wales at St. James's, who would obviously be brought up a Catholic. Doubts were cast on the authenticity of the birth, but one of the rites left over from the middle ages was that the birth of a child in the direct line of succession must be witnessed by a whole list of personalities, including, in Stuart and down to Victorian times, Gold Stick or his deputy. Thus it was that, when the Queen gave birth to her son – an event frankly unexpected –

among those present was Colonel Edward Griffin of the First Troop of Life Guards and Silverstick-in-Waiting, whose evidence, next to that of the physician, was held to be conclusive to the court of inquiry held by Chancery.

Thus William of Orange, disappointed, at any rate, of a crown for his wife, and urged by his London correspondents, put his plan for invasion in motion, and observers in London watched the Whitehall weathercock daily for signs of a 'Protestant wind'.

Chapter 3

William of Orange

WILLIAM of Orange was by no means the romantic deliverer of an oppressed nation, but a stout-hearted little Dutchman who set out to be the protector of protestantism in Europe against the might of Louis XIV. For this he needed the money and men of Britain, who hardly considered herself 'oppressed', although there were by now few doubts as to where his religion would lead King James II. Yet ordinary people were not seriously worried: they merely wanted to be left in peace, not torn by civil war as their fathers had been. Physically weak and unattractive, William was acceptable only so far as he could bring back James to reason.

There was no military reason for his easy triumph except that, unlike Monmouth, he came at the head of an army of 14,000 professionals, with the promised support of many of the country's leading figures, who could not afford to lose. James had an army that, although far superior, was torn internally by politics and religion. His finest soldier was John Churchill, whose loyalty was dubious: his army commander still the uninspired Feversham.

The course of what hardly deserves to be termed a campaign is well known. One of the few minor actions involved a party of the Fourth Troop of Life Guards under Patrick Sarsfield. They were intercepted near Wincanton by an Orange detachment under a Lieutenant Campbell, who challenged: 'Who art thou for?' 'I am for King James,' came the answer, 'And thou?' 'For the Prince of Orange,' replied Campbell.

'God damn me,' yelled Sarsfield, 'I'll prince ye,' and the Life Guards dashed in. The Royalists carried off the honours in the brisk contest, slaying nine (including Campbell) for the loss of four.

Senior officers, including Churchill, started a wave of desertions, and although the troops were still firm, James lost faith in his own cause. He drew back to the line of the Thames and then, escorted by his Life Guards, retired on London, sending his wife and son to France. He then made for the Thames estuary, leaving orders for Feversham not to resist the invader. At Sheerness he hired a ship but was taken prisoner by a gang of fishermen, from whom he was rescued by 240 of the Life Guard, sent after him by Feversham. London showed him how unnecessary his flight was as, escorted by Horse Grenadiers and Life Guards, he came home to Whitehall for the last time. 'The night,' it is said, 'concluded with Bells, Bonfires and demonstrations of Joy and Pleasure'.

William checked his pace at the news, but risked a further advance, whereupon James sank down in the dumps again and took off for France. Feversham interpreted the King's orders of 'no resistance' to mean a total disbandment of the Army, but William managed to stop the process: he needed every man for his fight against France. He took care to keep his Dutch Blue Guards around him, sending the Life Guards to country quarters, disbanding the new and suspect Fourth Troop. As an interesting sidelight it may be noted that the wooden chapel James had erected in the Hounslow camp for his Catholic troops was dismantled and brought to London, where it was the origin of the church which is now St. George's, Hanover Square.

Feversham and a few others were arrested, but the former was soon released at the instance of the Queen Dowager, who could not enjoy her nightly game of cards without her favourite partner! Many of the disbanded Catholic soldiers, especially the lifeguardsmen, made their way to Ireland to fight for King James and, when he went into final exile, helped to form the Irish Brigade of France. Among them was Partick Sarsfield who, created Earl of Lucan, commanded for James at Limerick and fell while fighting against his former comrades at Landen.

The new situation is summed up by the historian of the Household Cavalry: 'The Crown of England having been offered by a number of persons (who had no right to dispose of it) to two distinguished individuals (who equally had no right to accept it) the Glorious Revolution was complete. William and Mary were crowned at Westminster on April 11, 1689.' The three troops of Life Guards were assembled for the ceremony, and the Scots Troop was brought down to London for the first time. It was now to be more generally known as the 'Fourth Troop'.

William had plenty of work for his new army and the Second Troop of Life Guards were in Flanders that year. The troop took part, along with their future comrades of the Blues, in the highly creditable action at Walcourt under Churchill. But before William could settle down to his real task his own kingdoms must be brought to order. James had landed in Ireland and had raised, with French help, a considerable army. In 1690 the whole of the Life Guards and Horse Grenadiers crossed the Irish Channel and fought under William's command at the Battle of the Boyne. Tested troops now, content to serve under a monarch with no tendency to quit the field of battle, they fought their way through the remaining years of William's reign.

It was in June, 1691, that he opened his campaign in Flanders, accompanied by the Third and Fourth Troops of Life Guards and their Horse Grenadiers, preparing to meet the French under Marshal Luxemburg. There was a skirmish at Leuse, followed by an allied withdrawal, but by the following year William had a considerable force, including 23,000 British. Preferring not to trust Churchill, he put the British under Count Solmes, whose qualifications were modified by the fact that he hated the British as much as they detested him.

Luxemburg seized Namur and advanced on Brussels, but rested his army on the Senne at Steenkirk rather than risk a general action. The ground was unsuitable for cavalry and William wisely planned a surprise attack over ground which favoured his infantry. His preliminary bombardment lasted so long that Luxemburg had time to take precautions. The allied attack was spearheaded by the British infantry, entirely unsupported until the Life Guards came up on their right. Thirteen battalions stood up to fifty-three, plus seven regiments of French horse. The battle would have been William's had it not been for Solmes' refusal to reinforce.

'Let us see what sport these English bulldogs will show us,' he cried, and later: 'Damn the English. Since they are so fond of fighting let them have a bellyful.'

By sheer weight of numbers, and after standing a charge by the Swiss and French Guards, the British were forced back. The Life Guards were unable to get into effective action in the enclosed ground, but their Horse Grenadiers, dismounting for action as they had been trained, bore their share in the inevitable retreat. Solmes was censured in the House of Commons, and presumably damned the English once again.

The campaign of 1693 saw the high spot of the war in the battle of Landen, or Neerwinden. The Life Guards were in strength but were not brought into action until late in the day, for it was again largely an infantry battle. Luxemburg came up by a forced march on July 18. This day the scarlet lines of the British were prominent. Seven regiments of the Line formed William's right, with six more on the left and the Foot Guards in the centre.

Starting at dawn, the French withstood a four-hour bombardment before they were ordered forward. It was here, facing the Foot Guards, that Patrick Sarsfield, late of the

Life Guards, received his death wound. William led his own men in the counter-attack which flung back the French. The allies held their own everywhere, but were too weak to follow up their advantage. In six hours they had lost 4,000 men and now had to face the French Guard and the *Maison du Roy*. This onslaught of the élite impressed neither Coldstreamers nor Royal Scots and a private of the former took a colour before they retired in good order.

King William himself saved the situation, riding off to bring up the cavalry of the left – the Life Guards and five regiments of horse. The Duke of Ormonde, senior Life Guards' officer present, led the charge, but was wounded, dismounted and taken prisoner. The Life Guards met the *Maison du Roy* for the first time and were not disappointed at the result.

'Their cavalry,' admitted a French reporter, 'drove back the élite troops hitherto considered invincible. The Prince of Orange's Guards, with the Regiment of M. de Vaumont and two English regiments had this honour.' The King himself was in considerable danger. 'His Majesty is hurt,' wrote one officer, 'having led on several squadrons without his armour.' He was almost taken, but was rescued by Lieutenant Hatton Compton of the Third Troop, who rallied a few men for his protection and was promoted colonel on the spot. Thanks to the intervention of the cavalry the retreat was at least orderly.

The war lingered on into 1697, but there were no more set battles, at least not for the cavalry. The home-coming troops faced a savage attack in Parliament which was bought off by William sending his Dutch troops home. It is remarkable, incidentally, how many foreigners, mainly French Huguenots, were serving in the Life Guards (nearly forty per cent) and were now required to take out naturalisation papers. It was in William's reign that the Life Guards received a distinguished recruit – though he later found the pen a mightier weapon. He was Richard

Steele, famous essayist and son of a Dublin attorney, who joined as a private gentleman in 1694.

William's life was far from happy. He lost the wife he trusted, and became a sick man surrounded by plotters. One of the most dangerous was Sir John Fenwick, a lifeguardsman who resigned rather than serve the new régime, and who was later executed for treason. The Palace of Whitehall itself – the reason for the building of the Horse Guards – was burned down and the King moved out to Kensington. But the Whitehall Guard was convenient for police duties, and has therefore stayed where it first began.

Queen Anne succeeded in 1702 and two years later the Union of Scotland and England caused the Scots Troop to come south for good, bringing with it its Horse Grenadiers and being first stationed at Kingston-upon-Thames.

Much of the Guards' time was taken up by their duties in aid to the civil power, the most serious disturbance being the 'Sacheverell riots' of 1709. Doctor Sacheverell had preached an inflammatory sermon at St. Paul's and the Whig government was determined to condemn him. The trial lasted for some months, with the mob continuously on the streets. Matters became serious enough one night for the Whitehall Guard to be ordered out. Its commander, Captain Horsey, was a precise man and asked if he was expected to fight or to preach to the mob. If the former, well, fighting was his trade. If the latter, then they should send a trained speaker.

His doubts settled, he took off for the City, much to the detriment of the rioters. By sending six soldiers to secure the Bank, he helped to found the precedent by which the military were made responsible for the safe-keeping of the nation's finance.

Although the Life Guards had no direct share in the wars of the Duke of Marlborough, they still retained their old function as an officers' training corps, and many of their applications for commissions are on file. But at least one member of the corps served in his proper capacity – Trumpeter J. Seignier of the Third Troop, the Duke's trumpeter. Apparently he wore out one silver trumpet and the Jewel Office received the necessary indent for its replacement. The voice of the Treasury was heard when Godolphin endorsed the warrant: 'Query, what's become of the old one?'

Queen Anne's was a glorious, if often dangerous, reign. Her last military function was a review in Hyde Park of Life Guards and Horse Grenadiers, with six troops of the Blues and seven battalions of infantry. The first monarch of the new dynasty, King George I, was met at Greenwich by the Duke of Northumberland as Goldstick-in-Waiting, heading a hundred Life Guards and fifty Horse Grenadiers. As there was every likelihood of a Jacobite plot, the whole corps was drawn in from out-quarters and camped in the Park.

Chapter 4

Dettingen & Fontenoy

THE Life Guards had nearly half-a-century of peace – years that saw the consolidation of a Protestant monarchy in Britain, emphasized by the failure of the 'Fifteen' Jacobite rebellion in Scotland and the north-west of England. There was for some time a suspicion of Jacobitism in the Scots Fourth Troop, but the coming of the Hanoverians left the Life Guards comparatively unmoved. By and large the army had cause to be thankful to the first two Georges. Dull men they may have been, but they brought a deal of common sense into the Army, if only by finding some of its ways beyond the comprehension of their orderly minds.

It is possible to see during the reign of George I, the start of the deterioration which was to result, eventually, in the complete reform of the corps. Appointments as private gentlemen had, until now, lain in the monarch's hands, but George I allowed his prerogative to lapse, although his son resumed it. 'The King,' it was said, 'often tells Sir Robert Walpole he does not understand the Army nor who ought to be promoted there.' The new royal family did not make such wide calls for escort duties. They were by no means the travellers their predecessors were, and knew little of their domains beyond Hampton Court and Windsor.

Consequently a post in the Life Guard, if not quite a sinecure, was insufficient to keep a young man busy. Tavern squabbles ended too often in the first convenient garden, with drawn swords. The more industrious went in for trade on the side, so that in 1718 it became necessary for authority to take notice. There came an order that 'such of the Gentlemen of the 4th Troop of Horse Guards (com-

A Horse Grenadier of 1720.

By gracious permission of H.M. the Queen

manded by the Earl of Dundonald) as followed trades should abandon any such lay occupation within three months or dispose of their posts.' The *Evening Post* of August 7, 1718 carried a paragraph: 'Last Saturday orders came to the Troops of Guards that those who keep public houses etc. should either quit their occupation or the service.' It is evident that they had come down in the world. It is necessary to repeat that the Life Guards were as often referred to as 'Horse Guards' or simply 'The Guards', while the custom had hardened of calling the Horse Grenadiers, 'Horse Grenadier Guards'.

* * *

The War of the Austrian Succession, which opened in 1741, was fought to maintain a dull young princess, Maria Theresa, on her father's throne in Vienna. There were several rival candidates, the most important being the Elector of Bavaria. He was supported by France, Spain, Prussia and Saxony, the presence of the first-named on one side being sufficient reason for Britain to support the other. The odds were heavy enough, Britain only being sure of Hanover and the troops she hired from Hesse. The Dutch were lukewarm and Britain herself already had a war with Spain on her hands, in the matter of the loss of an ear by a sea-captain named Jenkins.

Frederick of Prussia got off to an early start, snatching Silesia from Maria Theresa. The French were in strength on the Rhine, with an occupation force in Prague. The small British contingent of the allied force assembled round Ghent, and was drilled to parade-ground efficiency during the winter of 1742/43 by John Dalrymple, Earl of Stair, a worthy if rusty veteran of Marlborough's army. King George II himself intended to take the field – was he not, too, a Marlborough veteran? Consequently the British included the Third and Fourth Troops of Life Guards and the Second Troop of Horse Grenadiers.

The Army was now becoming more literary and a good

deal of contemporary correspondence has survived. A series of letters addressed 'To Mr. Davenport, Aldgate', preserved in the Household Cavalry Museum, has been published by the Society for Army Historical Research. Now 'Mr. Davenport' was the brother of Richard Davenport, writer of the letters who, in 1742, bought a commission as sub-brigadier (2nd lieutenant) in the Fourth Troop and, with little or no qualification, shipped with his troop from Gravesend to Ostend and the war.

His first experience of active service was to get put under

General Richard Onslow inspecting the First Horse Grenadier Guards in 1742.

Painting by John Wootton. Property of the Beaverbrook Foundations.

arrest because a trumpeter had forgotten to sound 'To Horse', but then, as he explains, 'We are in the greatest hurry and confusion.' The Army was on the very point of marching and stayed excited most of the winter until February 1743. Davenport complains of draughty billets and bad cooking. The fact was that they were too apt to rely on innkeepers and were unfortunate in that, being gentlemen, such wives as they had brought with them were above kitchen duty. It might have been possible to hire from lesser regiments but, although their women 'looked like angels, they were, without exception that I ever saw' as drunken as their husbands. Our Mr. Davenport prayed for comfort for those who 'have wives or mistresses with them, which is near as bad as a wife'.

He did his training, learned to skate and tried his hand at a flirtation. Among his friends was George Augustus Eliot of the Horse Grenadiers, earning a little extra as a field engineer. Destined for fame as the heroic defender of Gibraltar, he must have been sad company, since he lived 'on a vegetarian diet and drank only water'. Davenport himself had an eye on extra pay when the job of adjutant became vacant; this brought an extra three shillings a day – and perquisites.

Things looked livelier in the new year. Frederick of Prussia, having digested Silesia, changed sides: the Dutch agreed to garrison the Austrian Netherlands and the army started its march to the Rhine. The Life Guards got as far as Brussels by March and stayed there until May. Davenport got his adjutancy – at a price – while Brother John in London got the contract for clothing the troop. Richard reminded him that 'the Adjutant is entitled to some advantage on these occasions'. His was a post to covet. He held two commissions, made a shilling a day on his forage allowance and took the field with 'two excellent servants, a strong cart and five good English horses'.

Brussels could not have been good for morale. Eliot

lived in a dirty house with a Flemish whore: Taylor, Davenport's other friend, got drunk every day. Between them and their servants they kept a 'little wooden shoes girl . . . but we begin to be jealous, having reason to suspect an intrigue between her and another officer or his servant who live next door'. But they were off at last, and by May 13 began the Rhine crossing near Coblenz.

It was high time the command made a decision. The King had arrived, but Lord Stair's mind was moving on a more ambitious plan than his. The old warrior proposed snapping up Dunkirk and then moving directly on Paris: but King George did not consider himself at war with France except as an auxiliary of Maria Theresa. He was not, indeed, particularly enthusiastic over the lady, except that the alliance was sufficient excuse for his having brought over a British force for the protection of Hanover, his homeland. He was already irritated in that he had been unable to pay his annual visit to the Electorate.

The Life Guards were learning that war is a stern business. At Hoescht they even had to sleep out – 'our Troop never having camped before'. Even the adjutant had 'three nights upon the ground, rolled up in my cloak' and existed on ammunition bread and a little bacon. His Majesty, like a wise monarch, travelled with thirteen Berlins, thirty-five wagons, fifty-four carts and 662 horses.

* * *

The battle of Dettingen was fought on June 16, 1743, and stands first in the list of Life Guards' battle honours. Except for the grant of 'NAMUR' given by William III to the 18th Royal Irish, battle honours were not granted to the British Army until 1784, when 'GIBRALTAR' was awarded to those regiments who took part in the great siege. Honours carried today for earlier actions were granted retrospectively.

King George and his allied army were literally forced into action, caught as they were on the north bank of the Main between Seligenstadt and Aschaffenburg, without supplies and under artillery fire from the other bank. By all the rules the 'mousetrap' set by de Noailles should have snapped shut, and ended the war with the King of England fuming inside. But Grammont, the advanced French general, attacked too soon and against orders. The Life Guards, when the battle opened, were in the first line of cavalry.

True to their main duty, the Life Guards detached thirty-six men as a personal guard for the King. They were early under fire, as Mr. Kendal, a private gentleman of the detachment, wrote home.

> 'They began to fire at him (the King) from a battery of twelve pieces; but as God would have it they levelled too high. I saw several balls go within half a yard of his head and our captain had his hat shot off; the man on my right had his horse shot and the man on my left was shot in the shoulder and the one next to him shot dead.'

The Duke of Aremberg tried to get the King out of danger, but the little man's blood was up and he saw the battle through.

His army, caught unawares and bunched up, was in danger of disaster and Kendal relates that 'the crying of the women and children frightened the King's horse and he ran away with him, but he soon stopped him.' He had all the courage of his race, and one account says that he dismounted after the incident, remarking that he could trust his own legs better!

The day was a famous one for cavalry, but the Life Guards chafed for a long time away to the right where they had been posted. At last a messenger spurred up to Crauford, commanding the cavalry of the right wing and newly-appointed colonel of the Fourth Troop. The rider pointed out the target – the French and Swiss Guards.

Crauford forbade the men to use their pistols and shouted to his trumpeter. Shrill above the din came the call: 'Britons strike home' and they were off, Crauford crying, 'This is fine diversion.'

Nothing could stand against their weight: French and Swiss gave way and there were no more to come – the battle was won, the French losses being swollen by the men drowned in the Main in retreat. Among the British casualties was George Augustus Eliot, whose horse rolled on him as he lay wounded. During the battle the baggage was plundered and the men lost all except what they carried on their saddles. They gained high praise, not only from their king but from that stern critic General Honeywood, who vowed he would 'never laugh at the Horse Guards again'. More to the point was that two men from each troop were granted commissions.

* * *

For the winter the Life Guards returned to Flanders and the King to England. Fighting in 1744 was confined to skirmishes; morale and discipline suffered; desertions increased. The adjutant lost his servant Sam – murdered by an absconding Horse Grenadier. To command his forces in Europe George II sent his second son, the Duke of Cumberland, who, in his impetuous twenties, was restrained (in theory anyway) by Austrian subordinates picked, it would almost appear, for their extreme age. But the Duke was not to be restrained. He marched off smartly to meet the French and, on May 3, 1745, found himself facing a superior enemy commanded by the finest soldier of the day, Marshal Saxe.

The foreseeable result was the defeat of the Allies at the battle of Fontenoy. But the British troops engaged had no cause for shame, which was more than some of their allies could claim. This action saw the first battle appearance of the kilt in the British service; the foundation of the reputation for musketry that served the Army so well and so long; and the famous meeting of the British and French Guards. Cumberland, if he was no great general, was an extremely brave one, moving in the smoke of battle on his grey Yorkshire mare, deserted by large units of his allies and the whole of his gun teams.

He has been criticised for not using his cavalry earlier and it is true that the major part of the Army sat fuming under fire for most of the day. But Sir James Campbell, its commander, had been struck by one of the first rounds of the enemy guns and, if he had orders, carried them off the field with him. The main force stood steady under repeated attack until early afternoon when, attacked on their right by the Irish Brigade of France and from the front by the Carabiniers and the *Maison du Roy,* shattered by four field guns which were run up to point-blank range, the weary British and Hanoverians gave way, sullenly and still unbroken.

It was then that Crauford, now commanding the whole of the cavalry, formed them into a protective screen and brought the survivors of the infantry off. There was no pursuit, Saxe admitting later: 'We had had enough of it.' Adjutant Davenport sent home a rain-drenched letter, suitably brief. 'After an engagement with the French of eight hours this day, I am perfectly well.' That they had been beaten scarcely occurred to him or his comrades.

'We don't allow it to be a victory on the French side,' commented Horace Walpole, 'but is just as a woman is not called "Mrs" until she is married, though she may have half-a-dozen natural children. . . . I pity the Duke, for it is almost the first battle of consequence we have lost.'

The war lingered on until 1748 but was over for the Life Guards who, with Prince Charles Edward now on the rampage, were needed at home. So seriously was the Young Pretender taken that King George loaded his yacht at Deptford and thought longingly of his ancestral home at Celle. The Life Guards arrived at Wilhelmstadt in December and sailed for Gravesend early in the new year. The passage home was worse than a pitched battle, for the Fourth Troop lost thirty-four horses 'by the unavoidable accidents of the sea'. But a worse fate was in store. Prince Charles Edward was now a fugitive and the Third and Fourth Troops of Life Guards, in anticipation of a general reduction of the army, were ordered to be disbanded on December 24, 1746.

Private Gentleman, Fourth Troop of Life Guards, 1742.
By kind permission of the Ministry of Defence

Advantage was taken by weeding out the first two troops, the vacancies being given to men of the disbanding junior troops. The Horse Grenadiers remained unaffected by the cut in the Life Guards. Indeed, their importance and the scale of their duties were increased thereby. Their headquarters were now permanently at the barracks in Charing Cross.

The old Guard House in Whitehall was overdue for rebuilding and the opportunity was taken to increase the accommodation scale. The first stone of the present buildings was laid in 1750, the architect being William Kent. The King performed a sort of opening ceremony the following year by driving through the arch. The privilege of driving through Horse Guards is still reserved for a very few people in official or court positions. The buildings provided accommodation for one hundred mounted men and office space for a growing military bureaucracy.

Under George II it was mainly the civil side of army administration that expanded into Horse Guards, including the Secretary-at-War himself. The Commander-in-Chief – when there was one – operated from Knightsbridge and later from Pall Mall, where Nell Gwynn once lived and where the Royal Automobile Club now stands. Incidentally, long before Big Ben and the B.B.C. were thought of the Horse Guards clock, still happily with us, set the time for London.

Chapter 5

Re-organisation

THE year 1756 saw an important innovation in the Life Guards, when they were given non-commissioned officers for the first time, bringing them more into line with the rest of the Army. The four senior 'right-hand men' of each troop became warrant officers with the title of 'quartermaster', while the four juniors were to be 'corporals of horse'. Quartermasters of cavalry came normally from the ranks, purchasing their warrants and providing their own horses and equipment. The corporals of horse were equivalent to sergeants in the line, as they still are.

The civil and social status not only of the Life Guards but also of the Horse Grenadiers is shown by the fact that, in the restricted franchise of the eighteenth century, many of them had votes – which they were expected to cast in the right direction. In 1774 George III was writing to Lord North: 'I have appraised Lord Delaware (commanding the First Troop) to have the Horse and Grenadier Guards spoken to for their votes: they have a large number.' Ten years later, when Fox was electioneering against Sir Cecil Wray in the Westminster constituency, Gillray published a cartoon with a telling caption.

'All Horse Guards, Grenadier Guards, Foot Guards and Blackguards who have not polled for the destruction of Chelsea Hospital and the tax on maidservants are desired to meet at the Gutter Hole opposite the Horse Guards, where they will have a full bumper of knock-me-down and plenty of soapsuds before they go to poll for Sir C. Wray, or eat. – N.B. Those who have no shoes or stockings may come without, there being a quantity of wooden shoes available.'

The King loathed Fox and 280 guardsmen were sent down to vote against him. Nevertheless he topped the poll. It should be noted that references to the 'Grenadier Guards' are to the horsemen of Charing Cross and not to the distinguished corps now bearing that title, which they did not receive until after Waterloo.

Court duty became a humdrum affair but the still-unpoliced state of the capital made the presence of the Guard at Whitehall the most important reason for the very continuance of the Life Guards. The streets were always dangerous, as in 1735 when the Countess of Stafford, returning from the Queen's drawing room, was stopped in her coach and robbed. The lady, understandably hysterical, returned to the palace and remained there until a detachment of Life Guards could be summoned to escort her home.

Matters assumed the proportions of civil war in 1780 with the Gordon Riots which, serious enough in themselves, served as a new pretext for the mob to take to the streets. It took not only the Guards, but twenty other regiments to restore order – and gave rise to the nightly Bank of England Guard still found by the Foot Guards. In June of the same year 'Lord Sandwich was the victim of a gross outrage, being torn out of his carriage, which was broken to pieces. He was badly hurt and rescued with difficulty by the Life Guards.'

* * *

It could all have but little attraction for the would-be soldier. Enrolment in the ranks of the Life Guards became a social stepping-stone for the sons of city merchants, so much so that the troops were known locally as the 'Cheesemongers'. The road led downwards into the first two decades of the reign of George III, culminating surely on the day when Queen Charlotte had to order her coachman to drive more slowly, two of her escort having fallen off!

Drastic change came in 1788, with the whole Army sadly shaken by events in North America. It was not only the Life Guards that were behind the times. The four remaining regiments of heavy horse had become almost museum pieces and were known as the 'Irish Horse' because they were stationed permanently there. They came home and were re-organised into Dragoon Guards. It was decreed that the Life Guards were to be transformed into two really regular regiments of cavalry, with their men enlisted normally and that the Horse Grenadiers were to be 'discontinued on the Establishment'.

It was in fact the Horse Grenadier Guards who survived. Their two troops became effectively the First and Second Regiments of Life Guards. Certainly places in the new regiments were offered to the private gentlemen, but few if any accepted such a serious job as real soldiering. 'The Horse Guards' as the Duke of York wrote, 'were little but a collection of London tradesmen.' They were refunded their entrance money to the tune of £24,000.

The Horse Grenadiers were men who had enlisted for the normal army period of 'life' and were therefore available for transfer. Recruiting posters of the period are usually flowery, but one of 1766 struck the right note in appealing 'for any young man of spirit and of a lively disposition, neat and well-made, who can have a good Character for his Honesty, now has an opportunity of being entertained as a Trooper in His Majesty's Second Troop of Horse Grenadier Guards.'

The new regiments had each an establishment of 230 of all ranks. It is presumed – if not entirely certain – that personnel from the First Troop of Grenadiers went to the First Life Guards and the men of the Second Troop went to the Second Life Guards, and the Second Troop of Horse Grenadiers was still accounted 'Scots'. This, coupled with the likelihood that some details of the Fourth, Scots, Troop of Life Guards went to the Second Troop on the disbandment of 1746, helps to account for the strong Scots tradition in the Second Life Guards which persisted, especially as regards officers, down to the amalgamation of 1922.

Even the Duke of York was mollified by the new set-up, although he might have been bold in posing, from the height of twenty-five years, as a military expert. But he *was* Commander-in-Chief (and Bishop of Osnabrück) and had attended the last manoeuvres of Frederick the Great. 'If the two regiments,' he wrote, 'keep exactly to the standard they have settled, they will be the finest bodies of men that ever were seen, the tallest not to exceed six foot one the shortest five foot eleven' a standard that was to prevail down to the Second World War. The full colonels were the Marquis of Lothian (though he soon lost his post on political grounds) and General Lord Amherst.

* * *

Barracks of a sort now existed at Knightsbridge, Charing Cross (to be given over to the Foot Guards) and in King Street, Portman Square, these last being leased premises. But these were little more than headquarters. The men's pay included an allowance for lodgings and they were only required to live within trumpet call. One set of orders set the northern limits for men stationed at Knightsbridge along the present Praed Street which, even in the relatively quiet London of the day, must have taxed even the strongest-lunged trumpeter!

When the new century opened, the Army was becoming more centralised. Life Guards recruits, at least, were being trained and fed in barracks. An indignant letter from the Barrack Office complained: 'The Plaistering of the Ceilings of the Soldiers' Mess Rooms was considerably broken and damaged, principally owing to the practice of drilling Recruits in the rooms immediately above them.'

The country was highly suspicious of barracks in general. Plans for the building of Regents Park Barracks to replace the leased premises near Portman Square were hotly debated in Press and Parliament. Mr. Huskisson lamented an 'attempt at something between a palace and a stable' – though generations of cavalrymen could never be brought to accept the 'palace' estimate. Mr. Freemantle was indignant at the thought of a 'Praetorian camp in London,' while *The Pilot* newspaper considered barracks as 'capable of being, if not altogether likely to be, converted into so many fortresses of the Crown, formidable to the Freedom of the People.' But 'freedom' could be liberally interpreted, particularly in London.

It has been made clear that the two new regiments, while retaining the status and prestige of the former Life Guards, with precedence over all other troops, were essentially the Horse Grenadier Guards and the regiment of today still remembers its direct ancestors in its uniform. The white pouchbelts carry a scarlet 'flask cord' which once secured the powder flasks of the Grenadiers. Before the amalgamation of 1922 these cords were red in the First and blue in the Second Life Guards. There is a further link in the grenade fastening at the throat of the officers' cloaks. When, in one period after Waterloo, the Life Guards adopted immense bearskin caps these, too, were decorated with the badge of the bursting grenade.

* * *

The strength of the King's Life Guard was reduced by a Gold Stick order of March, 1801. It was now to stand at three officers, one quartermaster, a trumpeter, two corporals of horse, forty-nine privates and fifty-five horses, with five mounted light dragoons attached. These last (known later as the War Office Letter Party) were

Trumpeters of the Life Guards in the 18th century were often men of colour.

By gracious permission of H.M. The Queen

continued down to 1914. They were provided by the line cavalry regiment at Hounslow and were all that was left of the chain of cavalry posts that carried the royal mail between London and Windsor.

The same Goldstick order summarised the duties of the guard. 'The King's Life Guard at Whitehall,' ran the order, 'being considered as a more alert duty than formerly, when it mounted once in four days and was more in the nature of an inlying picquet, the officers and men who compose this guard must hold themselves in constant readiness for the most alert performance of any duty, either of compliment or of actual service that may be required, without ceremony of previous notice.' The guard was required to post vedettes and send out regular patrols. Men not actually on duty might stretch their legs along either side of Whitehall and over the parade ground.

'Disturbances,' went on the order in sterner tone, 'having arisen in the Sutling House of the Foot Guards at the Tilt Yard between the men of the different guards, it is ordered that in future no man on the King's Life Guard shall go into the Tiltyard, the passage leading to it, or Sutling House of the Foot Guards on any pretext whatever.' The Sutling House was eventually shut down, after it had become the resort of thirsty civil servants!

It is usually imagined that the Queen's (or King's) Life Guard has always been the preserve of the Household Cavalry. Its very name is misleading: it is mounted at Horse Guards, it is called the Queen's Life Guard and for over a century and a half the Royal Horse Guards have shared in its duties. With the disappearance of the horse from the former cavalry regiments, it is unlikely that any other uniform will ever again be seen on duty in Whitehall. The last time a line regiment took the duty was in 1913, when the 18th Hussars came up from Hounslow to relieve the Household Cavalry for their royal review by King George V at Windsor.

During the Napoleonic wars line cavalry regiments made frequent appearances. While the Household Cavalry were serving under the Duke of Wellington in Spain or Flanders their depot squadrons were out at Romford, and London duty was carried out by any regiment available. In 1815 it was for the only time taken by a Yeomanry regiment – the London and Westminster Light Horse, an exclusive body raised in the City.

* * *

It is easy to raise a new regiment by a few strokes of a pen in an office, but the process takes time to come to fruition, so that it was fortunate that the two regiments of Life Guards had the strength of the Horse Grenadier Guards to draw upon, familiar as they were with London and state duties. Enlistment for life, which was the normal time, meant, in practice, for as long as a man could drill and use his arms. It is possible that many old grenadiers were still serving at the turn of the century, though it is unlikely that any of them survived to fight in Spain. Even there the cavalry commander complained of the age of the men.

In the early campaigns against the French the Life Guards took no part. They went steadily about their duties in London and drilled hard out at Wimbledon and Wormholt Scrubbs. It was as good a training as any other, especially for heavy cavalry as then understood. They were reckoned as the decisive weapon for shock action and would not normally be required to skirmish or find outposts. That was left to light dragoons or the new-fangled hussars. One thinks of the cavalry subaltern of an even later age who, asked to define the function of the cavalry, replied: 'To give tone to an otherwise sordid business!'

Chapter 6

The Peninsula

THE wars against the French Republic and Empire were the first to which the British committed themselves whole-heartedly as a nation. Communications (which meant news) were opening up, newsmen were more vocal and cartoonists reached the height of their venom. This had its inconveniences. Napoleon got his news of what was passing in Spain from the London press and Wellington complained bitterly of the more literary officers.

It may be imagined that the Life Guards writhed in impotence while great events unfolded in which they could play no part. It was small consolation to be told of the perils of invasion – and Boney did not come anyway. What was more infuriating, the Blues, for long closely associated with the Household Cavalry, were one of the first regiments to go, in 1793. The Life Guards had to wait until what seemed likely to be the final round.

There had been disasters enough, from the winter retreat of the Duke of York across the Netherlands and Germany, the terrible catastrophe which ended at Corunna and the appalling waste of Walcheren. There had been the mock peace of Amiens and then the nation settled down for a long war which would have seemed hopeless to most nations. At last the senior regiments got their chance when, late in 1812, a Household Brigade was ordered out to the Tagus. Life Guards and Blues had ridden together before, but never under this collective title. Two squadrons (all they could muster) were sent from each regiment, taking two peace-time troops to make one squadron. Each regiment received a third squadron before the war was out.

Wellington had not always been happy in his cavalry but he had not, until now, needed a great deal of it. His task had been to maintain himself along the rocky frontier between Portugal and Spain, and for this he relied largely on Craufur's incomparable Light Division, with its attached light dragoons. He was invariably outnumbered, but could rely on the normal jealousy between Napoleon's marshals which prevented them acting in unison.

Wellington understood the limitations of his cavalry well enough, particularly those of their generals, few of whom could handle two regiments together. One of them had tried his best back at Woodbridge, then the cavalry training area. The only result was that he got both 'armies' facing the same way! The cavalry commander in Spain was Sir Stapleton Cotton, a steady general who suited Wellington very well. He was noted for giving the best dinners in the Army and for being so well turned out that he was calculated to be worth £500 as he stood to any Frenchman who could capture him. Later, as Lord Combermere, he was Colonel of the First Life Guards for thirty-six years and gave his name to the cavalry barracks at Windsor.

Gallantry the cavalry had in full measure, but it could not make up for inefficiency. One most exciting charge Wellington described as 'the undisciplined stampede of a rabble' and threatened to dismount the offenders. Sword drill was so imperfect that troopers were apt to slice their horses' ears until Le Marchant, who was killed leading the heavy cavalry at Salamanca, took energetic steps to correct it. But the Army was now operating in Spain with its wider scope and Wellington needed more mounted men. He was now sent the 'Householders' and the Hussar Brigade.

The Blues had made their name in Flanders under the Duke of York and Wellington was, incidentally, their newly-appointed Colonel. The Hussars had done brilliantly under Paget during the retreat to Corunna: the Life

Guards – the 'Lumpers' to a tolerant Army – were the new boys among the Peninsular veterans.

* * *

They started off in leisurely fashion, taking six days from London to Portsmouth, one of them a rest day spent pleasantly at the Blue Bell and Blue Anchor, Haslemere and the Wheatsheaf and Flying Bull, Liphook. The First Life Guards embarked on October 24, 1812, and landed at Lisbon on November 30. They were lucky at that: one cavalry regiment lay for six weeks off Portsmouth, waiting for a wind. The horses had much the worst of it, crammed in the unsavoury holds of merchant ships. The Second Life Guards, having lost five horses on the voyage, landed with only 101 fit horses out of 243. Authority did what it could.

'The strictest possible attention,' ordered one commanding officer, 'must be paid to the rubbing of the horses' nostrils with vinegar at the first appearance of any indisposition and on most occasions of this sort they ought to be bled in the mouth until the arrival of the veterinary surgeon.'

Their first glimpse of active service was discouraging. In their naive enthusiasm many men threw away their grooming kits – and had to pay for a new issue. There was plenty to be done, both ceremonial work in Lisbon and in preparation for the campaign. Mules had been brought for baggage, camp kettles and forges, to the tune of sixty per regiment, plus one for each officer. There were the regimental women to be considered, although these were normally adept at fending for themselves. Sixteen wives came out with the First and eleven with the Second Life Guards.

Wellington was reputed not to care how his men turned out, so long as he could distinguish them from the French and that they carried their arms with the regulation supply of ammunition. But at Lisbon he seemed as exacting as the rest. Within days of landing they were warned for his review 'with helmets very clean,' while 'should the commanding officer for the future observe the slightest deviation in the dress of officers and men he will take the most serious notice of it.' One young officer was honoured with a special Brigade Order, the Major-General expressing his

The Life Guards' uniform for the war in the Peninsula.

'surprise at having yesterday seen Lieutenant Jervis of the Second Regiment of Life Guards wearing a forage cap in the Streets of Lisbon.'

Interior economy received due attention. Garrison Orders of December 8 were welcomed when the men read: 'The Deputy Commissary General will please to issue half a ration of wine or spirits as he shall find convenient, to the Brigade.' Tailors and shoemakers were busy and every horse was issued with two reserve sets of shoes, with 30,000 nails per regiment – a lesson learned the hard way on the retreat to Corunna. Many subsequent generations of soldiers will rejoice to note: 'The health of the soldiers is not to be impaired without any necessity by their being employed as Negroes or Pack Horses.'

* * *

Wellington's strategy for 1813 was the bold one of sweeping along the northern frontier of Portugal to strike at French communications with their homeland. His immediate aim was the elimination of Joseph Bonaparte, 'King of the Bottle' rather than of Spain. Joseph had 55,000 troops under Jourdain, very much strung out from the Douro to the Tagus, but capable of being reinforced by Suchet's and Clausel's 68,000 in Valencia and Catalonia. This Wellington provided against by remote control of a coastal campaign by British troops against Tarragona.

Spring was late that year and the Army could not march until mid-May, but the troops had been taking up positions since February. The Life Guards moved, crossing the Tagus at Abrantes and marching to Castello Branco. The men were living up to their reputation for good conduct and one commanding officer 'returned them his greatest thanks' after the civil authorities had reported their satisfaction with their guests. He even remitted a sentence of 400 lashes awarded one defaulter. Crime was, in fact, rare among them and another man, accused of picking a peasant's oranges, was acquitted on a plea of thirst!

The offensive was opened in three columns, the Life Guards marching under the chief's direct command to Salamanca, which was surrendered without argument. It was a comfortable billet, since the French had converted numerous religious buildings into barracks. The Second Life Guards occupied the Irish College, where the British had a friend in the Rector, Dr. Curtis, centre of an efficient intelligence service working for Wellington.

The advance was speeded up, the whole army being directed on Valladollid. The Life Guards crossed the Douro on June 4 and heard the mighty explosion with which the enemy prepared to quit Burgos, the important fortress which Wellington had once failed to take. The French plan was to hold the line of the Ebro, but Wellington outwitted them by moving the army to its left by roads so mountainous that they had never been thought practicable for an army. He crossed the river near its source and headed for Vittoria.

There was no fighting for cavalry in the mountains, but the Household Brigade kept well up. They were learning their trade fast and the condition of their horses was commented upon favourably. This was the more surprising since the majority of their mounts were three- and four-year-olds with little more than six months' service. For days they crossed mountains so steep that squadrons could only march in single file with the men dismounted. Once clear of the high ground the brigade went by the Bilbao road through the valley which pierced the Vittoria position.

The French formed for battle on June 19, but Wellington did not oblige them until the 21st. His plan depended upon a complicated approach march, the co-ordination of converging attacks and a strong flanking movement under Hill. The result was never in doubt, and Joseph's army streamed away without transport and with only one gun.

The Household Brigade was twice frustrated in its attempt to come to grips – once by a deep ravine and then by the headlong flight of the prey. The First Life Guards led the entry into the town itself.

The booty was enormous but most of it was looted by the soldiery. The painter Haydon tells of Corporal Sammons of the Second Life Guards, one of his favourite models, 'a soldier in every sense of the word. He would have brought a million safe and sound from Portsmouth to the King's mint, but he pushed his hand into King Joseph's coach at Vittoria and brought away a silver pepper box. He was an old satyr, very like Socrates in face, faithful to me, his colonel and his King; but let a pretty girl come in the way and the Lord have mercy on her.'

Wellington himself must be content with King Joseph's state sword and Marshal Jourdain's baton, which he sent dutifully back to England. The Prince Regent, ever gracious, wrote: 'You send me the baton of a Marshal of France. I send you in return that of England' – which was awkward, since such an article did not exist and had to be designed and made for the occasion. Far away in Vienna Beethoven wrote an overture based on '*Rule Britannia*',* while the Russians, for the only time in their history, sang a *Te Deum* for a foreign victory. The Life Guards had been in action for the first time since Fontenoy.

Far too late to be effective, General Clausel now came up to succour Joseph. A strong allied force, including the Household Brigade, drove him sharply back and the cavalry occupied Pampeluna and Logrono. Wellington's next obstacle was the barrier of the Pyrenees. He had moved his base up to the north of Spain and, after a difficult siege, had taken San Sebastian.

* * *

* '*Wellington's Victory*', an obscure piece of music written for a mechanical device called a panharmonicum, and scored for muskets and cannon. Other tunes included are the National Anthem and '*Malbrouck s'en va t'en guerre*'.

Quartermaster William Dobson, First Life Guards, and warrant officer of the reinforcement which now arrived from England, did himself reasonably well, despite some soldierly grousing. A letter of his dated March 13, 1814, to his wife in Little Russell Street, Bloomsbury was found, years ago now, in the cover of a book on a secondhand stall in Carlisle.

'I've got plenty of work, seven or eight hours on horse back every day,' he laments, 'and ever since March came in never had a fine day. . . . I've never been in bed since I left old England.' Later he reflected that things might have been worse. 'We live very well. We have tea or chocolate for breakfast and the Allowance of Meat and Bread, Spirits etc., as much as ever we can get through – The Troop is served with rum but I can draw either brandy, wine or what I chuse!' Then he struck a note that has been heard since in other campaigning days.

'I long to hear all the news at the old Detachment. There is a great many of them gets there wives with child all the way from Spain to England. Taylor Smith's wife is one: the Burning Buty they used to call her.' The spelling is his own.

There was little more work for the cavalry to do and the Life Guards saw a lot of Logrono and Pampeluna before they received the route for France. They crossed by the pass of Tolosa, the Seconds doing one march of eighteen hours without a halt. At the end of the campaign they were in reserve for the unnecessary battle of Toulouse, neither side having heard that the war was over.

War was conveniently forgotten, not the least by the French, delighted to play host, with champagne at a shilling the bottle. Captain Joe Kelly of the First Life Guards was much in demand at local concerts, having a voice renowned throughout the Army. He even produced a score of *God Save the King* for a town band. He was heard, two years later, singing for the Duke at a St. Patrick's Day dinner in Paris. His voice usually earned him a staff job, leaving the strictly military side to brother Edward of the same regiment.

One small-town mayor complained of the Life Guards wearing laurels of triumph in their helmets but was mollified by the explanation that they were oak leaves, not laurels, worn because they still remembered their founder, King Charles II, on his birthday. But they really did wear laurels a few days later, for the poor old King down at Windsor.

By arrangement with the Bourbon government, the whole of the cavalry marched clean through France to the Channel ports. The route for the Life Guards went via Toulouse, Monauban, Cahors, Limoges, Chateauroux, Orleans, Etampes, Nantes, Neufchatel, Abbeville and Montreuil to Boulogne, where they started to embark on June 21, 1814.

* * *

The war had not brought the Life Guards much fighting but they were different regiments from those who had joined the army on the Tagus. They themselves could now join in the laughter which had greeted their first 'action'. They had rounded up as spoils of war the grazing horses of an indignant light dragoon regiment and were putting in their claim for prize money while the dragoons were offering a reward for the capture of the thieves!

They had gone a long way. They were tried, active-service soldiers and experienced horsemasters. For the Peninsular soldier in general Napier provides the epitaph.

> 'When completely disciplined – and three years are required to accomplish this – his port is lofty and his movements free. The whole world cannot produce a nobler specimen of military bearing: nor is the mind unworthy of the outer man. He at all times proved that, while no physical military qualification was wanting, the fount of honour was also fresh and green within him.'

Chapter 7

Waterloo

SAFELY back in London, the First Regiment at Knightsbridge, the Second off Portman Square, the Life Guards settled down to enjoy the peace. The capital was *en fête*, decked out for the entertainment of allied guests before they took off for Vienna, where the jigsaw map of Europe must be made up again. Napoleon had been cut down to size to fit the miniature throne of Elba. The Life Guards, most unwisely, had also been cut down. They had with difficulty been able to take the field in 1812 and economy now tried to ensure that they would be unable to do so again. Meanwhile the bulk of Wellington's old infantry were engaged in a futile war in America.

* * *

The Second Life Guards had a hero of their own who, in sporting Britain, ranked almost as high as the Duke himself – Corporal John Shaw, of whom Dickens wrote later: 'Old Shaw the Lifeguardsman? Why, he's the model of the whole British Army in himself. . . . I'd give a fifty pound note to be such a figure of a man.' That was in the future: at the moment Shaw was hero of the Ring, heading for the heavyweight title, a left-hander, turning the scale at fifteen stone and standing six foot three. A lad from Nottinghamshire who, in a village bout, had taken the fancy of Jem Belcher himself, he had enlisted in the Second Life Guards in 1807, was taken up by the sporting officers of the Regiment and sent to train at the Fives Court, headquarters of the 'Fancy'.

Of seven major fights he won six and the *Military Magazine* recorded:

> 'He is very scientific and adopts the course of retreating and hitting successfully practised by Cribb. He fights with great good temper.' A later number described a 'desperate battle between Shaw and Burrow at Coombe Wood, thirteen rounds in seventeen minutes. . . . He beat his fourteen stone man till he could not see his way out of the ring.'

He was prevented from meeting Molyneux the Black but sent out a challenge to all England. The opponent selected was Painter, whom he met at Hounslow on April 8, 1815 and beat in half-an-hour, including ten knock-down blows. It is but fair to add that Painter had only that morning been released from the Fleet Prison, where 'training facilities were limited'. Shaw received an immediate offer for a new contest but, with all the dignity of his age, rejected the challenge.

'I should have been proud,' he replied, 'to have entered the lists against him but I find I am to be called upon shortly by my King and Country. . . . If I do, I consider it an honour to fall in their cause. However, if I am well, I will meet him on my return.'

* * *

Europe was aghast. Having disposed of the 'Corsican' it was now faced by the 'Emperor of Elba', who had contrived to outwit those appointed to watch him, landed with a few guardsmen in the south of France and rallied a discontented army to his Eagles. Louis XVIII retreated to the shelter of allied bayonets in Ghent and left the returned Emperor a clear field. The Congress of Vienna stopped dancing to take the field. It declared Napoleon an outlaw, set large but scattered forces in motion and appointed the Duke of Wellington (himself a member of Congress) its Commander-in-Chief.

Only in Belgium were field forces (partly British) in actual being, though Blücher, the old Prussian hussar, was soon heading in the right direction with a none-too-steady Prussian army. The main question in Brussels, full of British tourists, was: 'When will the Duke be here?' But when he came he saw little to content him. The British contingent contained far too many raw troops and his own government did not even call out the Militia until he urged it. There were Netherlanders whose allegiance was doubtful, a few second-line German units and some battalions and regiments of the ever-reliable King's German Legion, Hanoverian subjects of the King but integral units of the British Army. There was not a single British cavalry regiment.

The situation improved rapidly. The Militia was called out and drafted. Troops en route from America – that particular trouble having been solved – were rushed to Belgium. All available cavalry regiments were alerted, including a Household Brigade under Lord Edward Somerset. There was a stroke of luck in that, owing to the threat of labour troubles, more than the usual quota of cavalry regiments were in the Home Counties and on a service basis. One such was able to leave London in twelve hours fit for war.

Two squadrons of each Household Cavalry Regiment – just over 250 men per regiment – were all that could be made ready, although the paper strength of each regiment was increased to 589. To bring the brigade up to field strength four squadrons of the King's Dragoon Guards were added. The First Life Guards were commanded by Lieutenant-Colonel Ferrier, the Second by Lieutenant-Colonel the Hon. E. P. Lygon.

* * *

Through London they marched, via Greenwich to Ramsgate, shipping thence to Ostend, disembarking on

May 3. They had a brief glance at Brussels, then took up quarters in Meerbeck and Ninove. With them rode Corporal Shaw, potential heavyweight champion of England. To the rear of the First Life Guards rode Assistant Surgeon James who, in some measure the onlooker at the game, saw more of it than most and left his notes for the historian. Regiments and battalions had then their own surgeons and of them only those of the Household Cavalry remain today, together with the veterinary officers. In full dress they wear the uniform of their regiment, without the cuirass and with cocked hats instead of helmets. The surgeon has a black plume and the veterinary a red one.

* * * *

Of Wellington's seven cavalry brigades – there was no time to group them into divisions as Lord Uxbridge, the Cavalry Commander wished – six were extended in billets along the line of the Dender. The remaining brigade, under Dornberg, was deployed on the dangerous frontier. Dornberg was a competent German officer but had never served under the Duke and did not 'know the form'. The Duke had, in Colonel Colquhoun Grant – recently described as 'the first respectable spy' – the best intelligence officer in any army and had always relied on him in Spain. He now refused to make even a preliminary move until he had sure news from him as to Napoleon's intentions.

Grant did not let the master down and his report would have told Wellington all he wanted to know. But Dornberg, mistaking his role, took it upon himself to doubt Grant's accuracy and sent the report back for confirmation. The delay thus imposed enabled Napoleon to 'humbug' his opponent, to use the Duke's own expression. His loyalty to his one capable ally, Blücher, caused him to rush his troops up to an unprepared position with resultant casualties, rather than take up the position he had himself reconnoitred and which Marlborough long before him had selected as a possible battleground.

Once sure of his information and certain already that Blücher was too far forward, the Duke was almost exultant. While the 'sounds of revelry' surged in the Duchess of Richmond's ballroom, he took her husband into the small study where a map was produced.

'I shall fight him here,' he said, drawing his thumbnail along the ridge south of Mont St. Jean.

His immediate subordinates trickled away. Lord Uxbridge rounded up his own men, calling from the door of the ballroom: 'You gentlemen who have engaged partners had better finish your dancing and get to your quarters as soon as you can.' He wrote his orders at 11.40 pm on June 15, directing a concentration at Enghien.

As for the troops, if they were surprised there was no panic or disorder. It was what they had come for and Napoleon was, for them, a little man in a hat too big for him. The British among them had never met him, except for the rocket troop that had represented the British Army at Leipzig. There was advantage even in that, for the Duke himself gloried in the fact that he was that rarity – a general who, in meeting the Emperor, was not half beaten before the battle. He was more serene now: his cavalry was complete: he had most of the staff he had demanded and the infantry was still trickling in from America. Two thousand were on the march from Ostend even now.

James, the young Life Guards surgeon, has sketched the scene as the troops got under arms.

> 'It was a lovely morning, the sun about to rise and our trumpets sounding in every direction. I set off for Kelly's and as I passed down the back street met two hussars staggering along very drunk. One said to his companion, "I don't think I shall go to bed now." One of our lads laughed and called out, "Belike you will be put to bed with a shroud this night and know nothing about it."

'The First Regiment was ready but we were obliged to wait until half-past eight before the Brigade was collected. . . . We marched left in front and consequently the First was the rear regiment of the Brigade.'

The cavalry was asked to do the near impossible, regiments straining themselves to do nearly fifty miles to Quatre Bras, the point of contact between the allied outposts and Ney's advance. It was hardly more than a strong advanced guard that was holding up the impulsive Frenchman and the leading cavalry squadrons did not reach the position until 8 pm. Meanwhile the Prussians were being beaten soundly at nearby Ligny.

Too late to fight that evening, the cavalry were deployed next morning to cover the retirement of the foot, which Wellington was forced to order to conform to Blücher's involuntary retreat. The Life Guards emptied their hay nets and threw away the leathern stocks which were choking them on that intensely hot morning. Some files were at first dismounted to wait for the enemy, then the brigade withdrew to a position before the village of Genappe.

'A few of us,' wrote James, 'gathered in a knot and Kelly, ever generous, pulled a tongue out of his valise and divided it and some bread and a bottle of wine, which we drank out of Cox's little leather bucket.'

On the order 'The line will retire' they passed through the supporting German cavalry through 'fields of rye as tall as ourselves on horseback' and now with torrential rain adding to their difficulties. Along the narrow street of Genappe they went until they were halted on the outskirts. The Duke and his staff passed by 'smartly turned out in contrast to us who were beginning to show signs of a night in the open.'

The First Life Guards now stood in column, facing back down the road, among the last straggling houses.

'Captain Kelly,' James recalled, 'rode up to ask if I had

any gin in my case. Of this he took a sup and then said: "I should not be surprised if we had a bit of a fight here." ' He was right, for in front of them were two light regiments already engaged with French cavalry. The leading regiment, the 7th Hussars, were attacked by the Lancers of the Guard who overbore them, both by their superior weight and by the fact that the British had never met the cavalry lance before.

The next regiment, the 23rd Light Dragoons, showed 'little inclination' for the job and thus, according to James:

> 'Down poured the 7th Hussars and part of the 23rd, followed by the greater part of the French Cavalry, all in the utmost confusion. So utterly were they routed that men and horses tumbled into the ditches on either side of the road. The French pushed them so hotly that some of their dragoons were mixed up with our soldiers and one of them was killed by my side.'

Uxbridge, infuriated because the 7th, his own regiment, had left him alone within fifteen yards of the French advance, cried: 'The Life Guards shall have this honour' and so the big men on big horses, led by Edward Kelly, charged down the street. Kelly's own version was written to his wife on June 19.

> 'The First Life Guards,' he wrote, 'were halted and fronted to them'.Whale's squadron next the enemy who came charging in close column up the road in most gallant style with spears and flags in their front.
>
> 'Our men at first gave way and retreated a little when Whale was wounded by a Lancier in the back slightly. I left my squadron and went to the one next the enemy and charged the Lanciers twenty yards in front of my own men and although there were two of them at me at the time, I had the good fortune to kill their Colonel myself and one of the privates, when our Corporal Major came up just in time to save my life. Our charge was successful and we drove them back under their own guns into the village.'

An incident of the Waterloo campaign. Captain Edward Kelly, First Life Guards, having slain a colonel of French Cuirassiers, cuts off his epaulettes as a trophy.

Courtesy of the Parker Gallery

The Corporal Major was William Bishop, first of that rank in the Regiment, who was promoted quartermaster after the great battle.

Surgeon James remained at his post to the rear and

> 'soon saw the Regiment coming back, so covered with black mud that their faces were hardly distinguishable and the colour of their scarlet uniforms invisible. The ground was a quagmire and, if any man took a fall, he rose with a coat of mud from head to foot.'

Other men chuckled at the unusual appearance of the 'Hyde Park soldiers' and Johnny Kincaid of the Rifles spread the story that when a Lifeguardsman fell in the mud he went to the rear as being unfit to appear on parade: but then Kincaid was one of the Army's licensed jesters. Genappe was a smart affair, scarcely remembered in the light of greater events ahead. But for many years the First Life Guards celebrated Genappe rather than Waterloo, decorating their Standards with laurels on June 17.

* * *

The night was miserable – soaking wet, but Wellington had got his battle just where he wanted it. True to form, he held his main forces on the reverse slope of the slight ridge which marked the position, with advanced points occupying the garden and Château of Hougoumont and the farm of La Haye Sainte. Away – too far away – to his left, Blücher remustered his army to march with two corps to Wellington's assistance. The old man had had a tough time, having been unhorsed and then trampled on by his own cavalrymen. But, as he said: 'I have promised Wellington.'

> 'The dawn,' says James, 'found the army wet and miserable. The First Life Guards had bivouacked in a wood near some houses on the high road. Everyone was covered with mud and it was with the greatest difficulty that the men managed to get fires lit, some breakfast cooked and arms cleaned.'

In the early morning the troops were cheered by an issue of gin, the rain ceased and the Duke rode along the lines 'on his chestnut and with his staff, looking entirely unconcerned'. The sight of his long nose, old soldiers used to declare, was worth ten thousand men.

Corporal Shaw had a job to do, being sent with a detachment to collect forage. When he rejoined he just had time for a tot of rum before he fell in, in the centre of the left squadron, which was the left flank of the brigade. It was just turned 11 am when they stood to, to the right of the Brussels–Genappe road. The first guns opened at 11.30 am. The Household Brigade formed in mass: to their left, across the *chausée*, were the three regiments of the Union Brigade, Royals, Scots Greys and Inniskillings.

This is no place to tell of the heroic defence of Hougoumont, though the delay it imposed on the enemy was a major contribution to victory. This really was a battle when time was on our side. The Emperor's tactics were the initial attack on the Château with its threat to Wellington's lines of communication, then the shattering blow on the allied centre, weakened by bombardment. The British, he found, were singularly unimaginative. 'Shilling a day to be shot at' was the taunt of the London apprentices. They were 'shot at' now but realised, even as they fell, that their chief was giving them what protection he could.

'Hard pounding,' he remarked as he rode among the units of one division, 'we shall see who can pound the hardest.' He himself was everywhere: at one moment he had only one officer available on his staff.

* * *

It was 2 pm and at last the French drums beat *Old Trousers*, their *pas de charge*, a signal the veterans knew well enough. 'They came on in the old style,' explained Wellington later, 'and we beat them off in the old style.' The main French attack came in against the British line, which formed square when necessary. D'Erlon, with five divisions, tramped against and around La Haye Sainte. Mixed with them and to their left were the cuirassiers. The squares were swallowed and some of the younger allied units gave ground.

Lord Uxbridge, given a free hand with his cavalry, knew his moment. Dashing past Ponsonby with a shouted order for the Union to charge, he placed himself at the head of the Household Brigade and led them forward. The regiments formed line and moved stolidly over the ridge, steadying themselves and observing the dressing. The Second Life

Guards were on the left, K.D.G. in the centre and the First Life Guards to the right. The Blues, nominally in reserve, would not be denied. As the leading regiments opened out to engage on a wider front, they edged forward and lined up with the rest. The 'Charge' was sounded by Somerset's orderly trumpeter, John Edwards of the First Life Guards. He was a boy of sixteen, though he already had seven years' service. He served on until 1841, one of the last Waterloo veterans in the Regiment. He kept his field bugle, by permission, when a new pattern instrument was issued to the Army and it is still treasured in his regiment.

The Second Life Guards and K.D.G. swerved left of La Haye Sainte, brushed aside the Carabiniers and rode down Alix's infantry. The First and Blues took Milhaud's cuirassiers in mid-career and, despite the sharpshooters lining the hollow way across the main position, took no denial. French writers are apt to stress the importance of this farm track as an obstacle, though it presented small hindrance to the British horse.

Corporal Shaw went berserk, cutting down in this first charge nine Frenchmen, starting with a cuirassier whose face he sliced off 'as if it had been a piece of apple'. He knew what to do with cuirassiers, with their three inches extra in sword length. One must, he had told his comrades before the battle, come in at once and then 'smack at their faces with the hilt. They'll either topple or turn.' If the latter, they could quite simply be beheaded! Shaw's two flankers, Dakin and Hodgson, saw him dash at an Eagle, but he missed it in the general scrum.

It was, they remembered later, like the 'ringing of ten thousand blacksmiths' anvils'. Dakin, his horse dead, fought against two cuirassiers, also on foot, and 'divided their heads with cuts four and five'. Hodgson, a giant of six foot four, met an Irishman in the French service who roared, 'Damn you, I'll stop your crowing,' but the Life-guardsman slashed off the man's sword hand and then drove his own blade through the wretch's throat.

Of them all the Second Life Guards went furthest, getting through to the French wagon lines, where boy drivers sat to be slaughtered, tears streaming down their cheeks. The regiments were sadly scattered by now and made their way back in small bodies. Uxbridge remembered his real job and rode back to call up reserves – by now non-existent as such. Only Vandeleur could bring up his brigade to help the heavy cavalry out. But the two brigades had shattered an army corps, mauled two cavalry divisions, put fifteen guns out of action and taken two Eagles.

On the way back Shaw joined up with Kelly of the First and the two collected a detachment of their own men. Their way was barred by a whole regiment of Travers's brigade but they took the only way out – clean through the astonished Frenchmen. Hodgson, still by Shaw's side, split one man's skull and fairly decapitated another, the head, as he remembered, 'bobbing on his haversack,' which kept its bloody stain. As the brigade at last reformed (in single rank to make their front broader) the Duke himself gave ample thanks with his: 'Thank you, Life Guards.'

Their work was by no means finished, nor was Napoleon beaten. Time and again they rode out between the still defiant squares of their own infantry, returning to give confidence to the dwindling reserves. They were able to rescue the 5th Battalion of the King's German Legion – a unit which did not often need to be rescued. They even found time to laugh. Sam Godley was a trooper so bald that he was nicknamed the 'Marquis of Granby'. Like his famous namesake he lost his hat in one charge and his horse as well. Dismounted but undaunted, bald pate shining, he killed a Frenchman, took his horse and carried on, his comrades cheering: 'Go it, the Marquis.'

Corporal Shaw, in one detached action, found himself isolated, fighting against ten enemies. He accounted for five of them before his sword broke. Flinging the useless hilt in one man's face, he snatched off his heavy helmet and used it as a flail until he was cut down and left for dead. His final wound, according to Victor Hugo, came from the pistol of a boy drummer firing from a ditch.

At long last, with the Prussians coming up in force, the Guard itself beaten, Napoleon turned his back. Wellington and Blücher met at *La Belle Alliance*, while fifty files of the two heavy brigades were answering the roll. On a nearby dunghill, with the Prussian bands playing 'God Save the King', Corporal Shaw, the 'Milling Lifeguardsman' bled to death. His name and fame lived on. He even became a circus hero for, as late as 1843, a Mr. Powell at his 'Circus Royal' was billed to appear in his 'favourite role as Shaw the guardsman'. His skull was recovered from the battlefield and found peace at last in his own village church at Wollaton.

* * *

When all was done there was little room for rejoicing. In that army of comrades few had not a friend to mourn. They left the pursuit to the Prussians, who were eager enough.

'Well,' said the unemotional Wellington, 'thank God I don't know what it is to lose a battle, but certainly nothing can be more painful than to win one with the loss of so many of one's friends.'

Captain Edward Kelly sat up in bed for his letter-writing, having, when all was nearly over, been 'obliged to leave the field from a cannon shot having torn away part of the flesh of my right leg and driving the buttons of my overalls into the flesh.

> 'Now, my dearest love. I ensure you most solemnly that it is only a flesh wound and the Surgeon says he will ensure my being able to resume my duty in ten days. . . . I had three horses wounded under me and at last mounted a trooper who is also much cut in the head by the French cuirassiers who we also repulsed and beat twice off the field.

'I have now to tell you the most unpleasant part of the tale. The slaughter among us from cannon shot and shell was immense and a more bloody and dreadful field of battle was never seen. All my fine Troopers knocked to pieces, Ferrier killed, Lind killed, Whale and myself wounded, Colonel Fitzgerald, Second Life Guards and Major Boyce killed and Major Packe of the Blues killed.

'The officers and men of my Regiment are all pleased to bestow the most kind praises upon me and I consider myself fortunate in having been the first man in with the enemy in every attack we made.' And then, in a 'PS.'

'My beautiful bay mare was wounded in the head by a Lancier and I fear she is lost. She carried me beautifully in action and I would almost prefer being wounded myself to having lost her.'

He need not have worried. The mare recovered and outlived her master by six years. Her tail, together with other relics of Kelly, is in the Household Cavalry Museum.

The share of the Life Guards was heavy enough for two small regiments. The morning states of June 18 showed 243 and 248 men present. The revised casualty lists of the Adjutant General gave: First Life Guards – twenty-eight killed, forty-seven wounded: Second Life Guards – twenty-two killed, fifty wounded and sixty-three missing. The sting is in the final figure, for most of the 'missing' were in point of fact killed, stripped as they lay and buried unidentified.

Chapter 8

Age of Elegance

THE advance to Paris was almost a route march. Deserted by their Emperor, there was little to be seen of that talent for recuperation characteristic of French armies, though there was some resistance around Cambrai, and Grouchy's corps was still in being. Paris surrendered, not to the Marshal Prince of Prussia, nor even to Field-Marshal the Duke of Wellington, but to Drummer Wullie Ballantine of the 91st Highlanders, marching in with his flag of truce. Coming via Valençiennes and Cambrai, the Life Guards took up quarters in the city, finding patrols and guards on such unaccustomed beats as the Champs Elysées. They were not to see Paris again until 1919, when their Standards took the same route in allied triumph.

Routine caught up with them, most difficult for the First Regiment, which had lost its commanding officer, adjutant, orderly room clerk, two troop quartermasters and a full set of books. The temporary letter and order books still exist, with the labels of the French stationer from whom they were bought.

A campaign which had lasted three days was held responsible for a great many losses. The men had to pay for a complete new issue of leathern stocks, while every man wounded seems to have been admitted to hospital stark naked. It was useless to expect the two dead quartermasters to account for a complete month's pay for their men, but their replacements were stopped a shilling a day for twelve years to help their widows. Lord Harrington, the Colonel, drew the line at paying for eight farrier's axes, his agent remarking tartly that 'it might be supposed that

The years following Waterloo were times of pageantry in which the Life Guards played their part. A trumpeter, a trooper, a subaltern and a corporal of horse, painted by Dubois Drahonet in 1832.

By gracious permission of H.M. The Queen

the farriers were not engaged in any active operations.'

The Duke was back in his old form. In answer to a plea that the civil authorities should be made to pay for four horses missing from troop stables in Neuilly one night, came the reply:

> 'I am directed by the Field-Marshal to inform you that he would be casting a reflection on the Regiment to claim upon the French government for a loss which could not have been sustained had the precautions established by the Service been attended to.'

But the First Life Guards did get back the grey mare Colonel Ferrier was riding when he was killed. It had been caught by a dragoon, sold for ten Napoleons to an officer of the 28th, sold again to another of the 26th and returned at last to the Regiment.

Hardly had the smoke of battle settled when, 'His Royal Highness the Prince Regent declares himself Colonel-in-Chief of the Household Cavalry as a mark of his august appreciation of their gallantry at the Battle of Waterloo.' Shortly afterwards – and probably for the same reason – a consignment of crowns was sent from England to be worn above the stripes of the N.C.Os. in undress, a custom which has continued. No change was made in full dress on which no chevrons are worn, rank being marked by the wearing of golden aiguilettes, on the right shoulder for officers, the left for N.C.Os. With the exception of Queen Victoria, every monarch since George IV has been Colonel-in-Chief of the Life Guards and Royal Horse Guards.

* * *

There was never an age in which Britain set the pace of European life as that which followed Waterloo and lasted throughout the century. It was especially an age of elegance, with the Prince Regent, later King George IV, as the 'First Gentleman of Europe'. From 1815 to 1881, the Life

For a few years in the 1830s, this most unusual uniform was worn by the Kettledrummer of the Second Life Guards.

Painting by J. Fearnley *Photograph by Capt. A. C. Cooper*
Published by permission Officer Commanding Household Cavalry

Guards, with their comrades of the Blues, shone in splendour in the precincts of a court whose orbit was London, Windsor and Brighton. They were the setting for the jewel of the Monarchy.

Brighton became a subsidiary capital and the Life Guards knew it well. 'During the period of His Majesty's

This picture of a trooper of the Second Life Guards VIII shows the enormous bearskin cap first worn for the coronation of King George IV. This, together with the grenade ornaments, recalls the Horse Grenadiers from which the Regiment was recruited in 1788.
Oil painting R. Walker, c. 1835 *Courtesy the Parker Gallery*

residence,' ran an order of 1822, 'officers are required never to appear in the Town otherwise than in Full Dress.' There were niceties even in this, for: 'Should His Majesty be graciously pleased to invite any officer to the Pavilion, he is to wear in place of the Aiguilettes and straps the Aiguilette and Epaulettes.' It was a golden time for military tailors such as Mr. Andrews of Pall Mall and Mr. Stultz of Clifford, for uniforms were changing constantly.

There were experiments with hats: cocked hats with feathers, Roman and Grecian helmets (abandoned because their wearing in a high wind was positively dangerous), and enormous bearskin caps. Cuirasses, never worn since the reign of King William III, were reintroduced, the First Life Guards cleaning up those they had dutifully held in store for over a century.

Critics were sarcastic.

> 'Who,' asked one, 'were the persons who devoted their time to the mode of sticking ostrich feathers in hats? They should rejoice in an acquaintanceship with the military milliners who had tried to transform the Life Guards.' Another wrote:
>
> 'Those Gallant Corps who on the Plain of Waterloo decided the fate of Europe have had, we understand, one allowance granted to them lately, *viz* that they are to change their uniform four times a year only . . . as the Royal Tailor has signified that, if more frequent changes took place, he should not think himself quite so sure of being paid.'

But they still had duties more serious. Peace brought its troubles. The introduction of machinery, the running down of war industries and the wholesale discharge of soldiers, swelled the ranks of the unemployed. London, as ever, was prominent among the trouble spots. The Life Guards became the 'Piccadilly Butchers', although the better-informed were sometimes amazed at their tolerance under provocation. Possibly the Metropolitan Police are their true successors.

There was one serious plot for revolution (the Cato Street conspiracy) which caused the Duke of Wellington to plan a complete campaign for the defence of London. Nightly patrols were sent out from Knightsbridge, Portman Street and Horse Guards. But, as is usual with plots, someone talked, and for the last time lifeguardsmen escorted malefactors to the Tower. Previous trouble in the City itself caused the Second Life Guards to answer an appeal from the Lord Mayor, when they were quartered in inns on both sides of the river. 'The Life Guards,' ran the account, 'conducted themselves with great propriety, striking with the flats of their swords only, left and right.'

The funeral procession of Queen Caroline, George IV's foolish and deserted wife, was the occasion of serious riots. She died at Hammersmith and was to be buried in Germany. The London mob had always supported her and were determined to do so to the end. To avoid trouble the procession was routed via the northern suburbs to the docks, but the population thought otherwise. The Blues found the first escort but at Kensington Gate, where they should have turned into the Park, the way was blocked. The Life Guards now arrived from inside the Park and there was a free-for-all until the magistrate in charge decided the procession should go along Knightsbridge.

There was a barricade of wagons at Hyde Park Corner but the Life Guards dismounted and thrust it aside. Similar obstacles at Cumberland and Tyburn Gates forced the cortège along Oxford Street, after the Life Guards, at the end of their patience, opened fire and killed two rioters. The dead Queen was received with ceremony and escorted through the City. A coroner's jury returned a verdict of 'Manslaughter against the officers and men of the First Regiment of Life Guards' but in more enlightened quarters a subscription was taken up for the men of the Regiment, who made it over to the Duke of York's School.

King William IV made little impact on military affairs,

but in 1831 presented the two Regiments of Life Guards with the silver kettledrums they still carry. Regimental bands were now being developed, that of the First Regiment appearing in the state parades of 1822. At least one attempt was made in that regiment to train a negro kettle-drummer, with the sad result that Josiah Uzabb, native of Martinique, ('Complexion Black') had to be discharged, 'in consequence of his not being able to learn to beat the drum'. Army musicians were often men of colour and a little later the Second Life Guards were justly proud of their four black trombonists.

* * *

In 1821 the three regiments (the Blues having taken their rightful place as full members of the Household Cavalry) started their regular rotation of quarters, two regiments always being in London with the third at Windsor. London duties were heavy but were lightened considerably during the long widowhood of Queen Victoria. It was hardly thinkable for royalty to move about without an escort, even for their own amusement. Escorts for gala performances at the theatre were continued even into the present century.

In 1827 the regiment at Hyde Park Barracks was finding a King's Life Guard of fifty-one every alternate day, a barrack guard of twenty and an inlying picquet of twenty-one daily. In addition, if the King was in London, a patrol of four men was sent round St. James's Park every evening. This was, of course, in addition to incidental escorts.

Early in the second half of the century the whole of the cavalry was re-organised. The old troops were largely administrative, the normal field organisation being the squadron. It now became the real sub-division of the regiment, two of the old troops going to form one new squadron. The corporal majors, who had replaced the troop quartermasters, became squadron corporal majors and squadron quartermaster corporals. Each of them wore four stripes reversed on the cuff, surmounted by the usual crown of the Household Cavalry. It was not until 1915, when warrant officers class two were introduced into the Army, that the squadron corporal major wore the crown alone as the badge of his rank.

Only sixteen full corporals were allowed per regiment and there were no lance corporals until 1920. This being quite insufficient for duty, regiments appointed as many 'acting corporals' as they found necessary, all wearing, as lance corporals do today in undress, two stripes and a crown. These aspiring young soldiers started off up the ladder in debt, as they were required to find aiguilettes at their own expense. Today they wear a modified aiguilette at public expense.

The Army was left very much to its own devices as far as

Landseer rarely attempted a military subject. This sketch of Queen Victoria and the Life Guards was made in 1838.

From a private collection

welfare was concerned, but had a powerful friend in Queen Victoria. She came out strongly in favour of married quarters and, after a private attempt had been made by Guards officers in London, sponsored some of the first built-in barracks at Windsor.

* * *

Soldiering in the second half of the century was still a most expensive hobby for officers. One officer in the Second Life Guards recorded that his first set of uniforms alone cost him 600 pounds – and that when the pound was really 'sterling'. Uniform included – as a bare necessity – two tunics, two stable jackets, frock coat, patrol jacket, mess dress, cloak and cape, with all the accompanying straps, belts, trouserings and boots. Two black chargers, with their saddlery, set him back still further. His pay was a mockery; but he had the consolation that discipline was fairly easy, as it had to be when he could 'put in his papers' if displeased with his colonel or adjutant!

'A cavalry soldier is no damned use unless he swaggers,' was a favourite dictum of one drill corporal major of the Seconds. Colonel Ewart of that Regiment, later to command the Household Cavalry in Egypt, was described as 'swagger incarnate'. The description of him went on: 'His clothes, his cigars, the chestnut team he drove in his coach, his social aspirations, were eloquent of a devout belief in himself.' But he was not quite up to the form of another lieutenant-colonel who rode his regimental charger into Poole's to demonstrate on the spot that his riding pants were not up to standard!

It was Edward, Prince of Wales, appointed Colonel-in-Chief of the Household Cavalry in 1880, who got the vexed question settled as to the respective status of Silver-stick-in-Waiting and the Field Officer-in-Brigade-Waiting of the Foot Guards. Lord Esher, Master of the Rolls, was appointed to hear evidence from both sides and came down in favour of Silverstick. This officer, as deputy to Gold Stick since the reign of Charles II, was personally responsible for the safety of the Monarch, while the Foot Guards officer had the purely military duty – since the reign of Queen Anne – of conveying the Sovereign's orders to the Brigade of Guards. What it meant in practice was that the Household Cavalryman rode near the right-hand wheel of the carriage with the Foot Guard to the left and also took precedence when dismounted. The senior officer of Household Cavalry present on parade, whether Gold Stick or Silverstick, is the military officer closest to the person of the Sovereign.

Victorian soldiers changed quarters generally once a year and did so as they would have marched on active service, as in this picture of the Second Life Guards arriving at Regents Park Barracks in 1862.

Chapter 9

Up and Down Africa

THE last two decades of the nineteenth century broke the peace which the Life Guards had observed since Waterloo. In these decades the Regiment saw Africa – then the 'Dark Continent' – from both ends. There were wars enough in the interim, but Queen Victoria had decided views as to the propriety of committing her closest guards in what she saw as minor squabbles. That the Life Guards took part in two wars at the eastern end of the Mediterranean was due primarily to the vehement urging of the Prince of Wales, their Colonel-in-Chief. His own soldierly instincts had been frustrated, save for a casual attachment to a battalion of the Grenadier Guards on the Curragh. Even now he was refused permission to take the field in person, though it was difficult to see in what capacity he could have been employed.

The actual right of the Household Cavalry was obvious, keen commanding officers having raised the efficiency of the regiments to such a pitch that they could no longer be denied. James Keith Fraser was gazetted to the First Life Guards in 1852, seeing much duty on the staff and serving in the Crimea. When he came to command his regiment in 1877 he set out to shatter the illusion that the Life Guards were merely show troops. When a composite regiment of Household Cavalry was ordered east in 1881 it was his right, as senior lieutenant-colonel, to command it. But the sailing of the Regiment was postponed by a fortnight, during which his period of command expired. Red tape took over and frustrated his just ambition.

Slightly younger than Keith Fraser was Lord Cochrane (later Earl of Dundonald), who joined the Second Life

The Earl of Dundonald, Commanding Second Life Guards, was among the first to realise the potentialities of the Maxim gun, and invented a 'galloping carriage' so that it could go into action with the Regiment.

Guards in 1870. Much of his career can be anticipated here. At Abu Klea he led the Second Life Guards detachment of the Heavy Camel Regiment. He was so far ahead of his time as to consider the rifle mightier than the sword. Cavalrymen were allowed a minimum of practice ammunition but Dundonald, when he came to command in 1895, with his officers, bought ammunition for the Regiment and paid the fares to Bisley for regular practice. With the machine gun in its infancy, Dundonald developed a horsed carriage so that the weapon could go into action with its regiment.

The Second Boer War caught him on half pay, but he sailed at his own expense and got command of a scratch brigade in Natal. It is significant that three of his officers became field-marshals – Captains Hubert Gough and William Birdwood and Lieutenant-Colonel the Hon. J. Byng. Later he re-organised the Canadian Militia, with notable results in 1914, and inaugurated the present practice of affiliating Imperial and Dominion units. He was full colonel of the Second Life Guards from 1906–1919. Until he died he kept close touch with his old regiment so that, even after the amalgamation of 1922, the N.C.O.s were still attending the Derby at his expense and smoking the 'Dundonald Cigars' at Christmas.

* * *

Stripped of all diplomatic frills, the Egyptian War of 1882 was fought for the control of the Suez Canal, in face of French opposition and the ungracious attitude of other powers. 'Egypt,' proclaimed the Queen, 'can be in *no other* hands than ours if she is to be taken from Turkey, or rather from the Khedive.' The immediate reason for the war (a good one in any case) was provided by serious rioting in Alexandria on June 11, when a hundred Europeans were slaughtered and the British Consul dragged from his carriage. The instigator of the trouble was an ambitious colonel named Arabi Pasha.

Those were the days of 'gunboat diplomacy' and the Admiralty moved swiftly to bombard Alexandria on the plea of protecting the fleet anchorage. Their Lordships now let their imagination run riot, demanding that soldiers should be placed under their command for the protection of key points. Sir Garnet Wolseley, Adjutant General and the leading British general of the day, drew the line at this and a full-scale military expedition under his own command was mounted instead.

The General was far from enthusiastic that a Household Cavalry regiment should be included in his force. He was against the 'big men on big horses', particularly as they provided a powerful argument against his pet scheme for a short-service army capable of rapid expansion. He was overruled, not least because he was no favourite of the

Queen. A composite regiment of Household Cavalry was sent out under Colonel Ewart, Second Life Guards. It was all they could send from a peace-time strength of four hundred per regiment, including recruits and without any reserve at all.

The Regiment landed in August 1882 and was brigaded with the 4th and 7th Dragoon Guards under Sir Baker Russell; the cavalry division, which included a brigade from India, being commanded by Sir Drury Lowe. It was the last time that a distinction was to be made between 'heavy' and 'light' brigades. The brigade was in action almost as soon as it landed; at El Magfar, Mahmasal and the Kassassin Lock of the Freshwater Canal. This last was a weak position held by less than 2,000 troops, with the cavalry four miles away. It was attacked on August 28 and by evening the position had become awkward enough for the cavalry to be called up.

The men of the Household Cavalry with the 7th Dragoon Guards and part of 'N' Battery, R.H.A. came in after the sun had set. They swept round Arabi's left flank in bright moonlight, being received with a hurried but heavy discharge of all arms. 'N' Battery unlimbered and opened fire; it was the moment for decisive action and the Household Cavalry, headed by the Brigadier and Ewart, drove home in the celebrated 'Moonlight Charge,' which, to quote the official report, was 'right gallantly led and executed. The enemy's infantry was completely shattered and our cavalry swept through a battery of seven or nine guns.'

Lord Wolseley has left it on record that the heavy swords of Life Guards and Blues were frequently used to such effect as to cleave opponents from head to waistline. 'Their excellent behaviour at all times,'[1] he wrote, 'is on a par with their gallantry in action,' admitting that they had taught him a lesson. The force was not entirely assembled until September 12 and there was sharp fighting in the meantime. The assault on the main enemy position of Tel-el-Kebir

Sir George Arthur, later historian of the Household Cavalry, recorded that the initial expense for uniforms to a subaltern of the Life Guards was £600. This 'Spy' cartoon shows him in one of the many orders of dress.

was mounted with the cavalry on the right of the line. It was a drill book operation: a dawn attack by infantry, then the charge and pursuit by cavalry, followed by a dash of thirty-nine miles on Cairo itself which put the Khedive back on his throne.

Whatever her personal feelings with regard to her Commander-in-Chief, the Queen stood behind him against her other *bête noir*, Gladstone. She insisted on the 'vital importance of not interfering with or directing Sir Garnet Wolseley's movements. Meddling from home, especially by civilians, might be, to say the very least, injurious.' The General's praise of her Household Cavalry delighted her, particularly as she was able to point the moral.

'The Queen is glad to hear,' she wrote, 'that Sir Garnet Wolseley entertains such a high opinion of her Household Cavalry; she would remind him that they are the only Long Service Corps in the Army.'

Modern pressmen would speak of a 'police operation' but in 1882 the short effective campaign caught the imagination of Fleet Street and nation alike. There were scenes of wild enthusiasm when the victors came home. The First Life Guards rode through decorated streets to Knightsbridge, where they were received by the Prince and Princess of Wales. The Mayor of Windsor presented an address to the Second Life Guards. Count Munster, the observant German Ambassador, reported home that the Household Cavalry horses returned in better condition than the rest.

The campaign put paid to scarlet and blue as battledress. For the first time Indian troops fought alongside British troops west of Suez and they had impressed observers with the practical advantage of their khaki uniforms. The Duke of Connaught wrote home in favour of the new colour and, although the Queen was scornful of the 'sort of *café au lait* colour' she gave way in the end.

Trouble in the Nile Delta had been preceded by trouble upstream in the Sudan. Egyptian forces, even under British officers, were not of high quality and the Khedive's control of the Sudan was ineffective. Mahomet Ahmed, self-proclaimed Mahdi of Moslem prophecy, was in arms. Matters had been allowed to drift and, by early 1884, were obviously desperate, not the least for General Gordon, British commander in Khartoum, the Sudanese capital.

Gordon had been sent not to fight, but to organise the inevitable evacuation of Khartoum. A popular national hero with a deserved reputation for personal gallantry, he lacked some of the plain military efficiency the situation called for. Even his departure from England was a trifle muddled. He arrived at Victoria hours too early and without a penny in his pocket. A friend who knew his failings came prepared with a bag of sovereigns, while another bore him off in a cab to Knightsbridge for the dinner he had forgotten to eat. A silver plate in the old mess room recalled the fact, but even that was wrong since, not being 'dressed', his meal was brought to him on a tray in the ante-room!

His isolation at Khartoum resulted in a public outcry and the government was forced to organise a relief force, again under Wolseley. The campaign seems, in retrospect, like a Hollywood story lacking a heroine. There were two distinct relief forces. One was taken up the Nile in tourist steamers as far as they could go, then transferred to Canadian canoes complete with *voyageurs*. The second was to cross the desert on camels which, to most of the men affected, were creatures out of a zoo.

The river expedition was mainly made up from men already in Egypt, but three of the four camel regiments came from England, raised by drafting small bodies of picked men from many regiments. Each regiment of Household Cavalry supplied forty men to the Heavy Camel Regiment, commanded by Colonel the Hon. R. Talbot, First Life Guards. The scheme was open to many objections, some forcibly expressed, but Wolseley had his way.

The Heavy Camel Regiment was inspected by the Duke of Cambridge (one of the most strenuous objectors to the whole scheme) on September 24, 1884 and embarked two days later on the *Deccan.* There had been no training possible and the men were not impressed by their mounts when they got them at Assuan. The force was assembled under Sir Herbert Stewart at Korti and set out on its forced march on December 30, one day before Gordon's last message: 'All right' came into camp.

One hundred and fifty miles of desert faced them, without tents or baggage and covered by a slight force of horsed cavalry. Marching in square, all went well until they reached the wells of Abu Klea, three-quarters of the way out. There, on January 17, 1885, the square was attacked at odds of eight to one by a horde of dervishes, just as it was closing in. The tribesmen poured through a gap, but discipline told and every enemy that penetrated the square was killed, with a loss of over 1,000 against the seventy-four casualties in the British force.

Two days later they sighted the Nile but had to fight their way to the bank. Now came news of Gordon's death and the desert force retraced its steps. The much-vaunted camels were exhausted and the men limped back to Korti on foot. Severe losses had not undermined morale and a new advance was proclaimed for the autumn. But the tune was called from London and the Sudan was left to its own devices until, in 1898, Lord Kitchener avenged Gordon.

The principle of a composite regiment of Household Cavalry having been established, it was applied again to the Second Boer War. A Household Cavalry reserve was not established until 1904, after which men enlisted for eight years with the Colours and four with the army reserve. Even then the tendency was for men to continue in the service up to the full term of twenty-one years.

The Boer War is often condemned as 'imperialistic' but

the plain fact was that in Boer and British colonials two distinct civilisations were opposed. The Cape had been acquired during the Napoleonic Wars and largely developed by British enterprise. The Boer was normally a farmer and, as the towns and their industries advanced, he trekked north in a vain attempt to stick to his own way of life. The discovery of mineral riches had not helped, bringing in capital and labour of far from uniform quality. One of London's bitter jokes during the war was that, while the pick of the British were being shot in South Africa, the pick of the South African millionaires' wives were being hung in the Royal Academy.

Britain entered the war, after her fashion, light-heartedly enough, her soldiers rhymed by Kipling, their wives supported by public subscription. The men found that the Boers were not the straw-chewing farmers they expected, but tough fighting men who scorned many of the rules, but could ride and shoot with distinction. It took the efforts of much of the Empire to subdue them.

> 'The Boer War,' says a recent writer,' is said to be the conflict which saved Britain in 1914, hauling the British Army into such a state of preparedness which it would have been unlikely to have achieved otherwise. And that's the only good point about it.'

Wars were now becoming public property, aided by the new popular press and the improvement in communications. It was such advantage that gave rise to the breed of arm-chair generals to be found in their perfection in the London clubs. Sometimes they even had a vague claim to knowledge; on one occasion Sir Redvers Buller, home from the front and sitting at the long table in the Beefsteak, was heard to protest: 'There's no animal on God's earth like a militia colonel.'

The new Household Cavalry Composite Regiment mobilised at Windsor, where the Queen herself saw them off. It was commanded by Colonel Audley Neeld, Second Life Guards, with Colonel T. C. P. Calley, First Life Guards as second-in-command. Landing at Cape Town at the end of December, 1899, it was brigaded with the 10th Royal Hussars and the 12th Prince of Wales's Royal Lancers. Things were going badly, with British forces besieged at Ladysmith, Kimberley and Mafeking.

The Brigade joined Sir John French's force for the relief of Kimberley. Three brigades of cavalry, two of mounted infantry, seven batteries of Royal Horse Artillery, together with colonial units and auxiliaries, were assembled and lined up along the Modder River. Sir John and his men swept out of camp on February 11, 1900: Cronje was outflanked and out-manoeuvred and three thousand sabres galloped three miles through the defile between the two main enemy positions. Kimberley was saved in four days and 'Johnny' French was the Army's hero.

Cronje, realising that the real British objective must be Bloemfontein, made off to the east but French, anticipating him, detached Broadwood's brigade, which intercepted him and held him until French was sufficiently reinforced to fight the brilliant action of Paardeberg, as the result of which Cronje surrendered.

Mobile columns were now sent out in all directions and guerilla warfare, with all its disadvantages to the regular soldier, became widespread. Returning from one drive into hostile country, the Household Cavalry was involved in the disaster of Sanna's Post, where, at a ford over the Modder, Christian de Wet had laid an ambush. Tired after a night march, the brigade and the convoy it was escorting had just commenced the crossing when de Wet pounced. The lumbering ox waggons were jammed in the ford and the two R.H.A. batteries were involved in the confusion, losing six of their twelve guns. Broadwood set up a fire position back from the river with 'Q' Battery and Roberts's Horse, and sent first the 10th Hussars and then the Household Regiment to outflank the Boers at an upstream drift. But the loss of the guns made the position insecure and Broadwood, having lost 600 men out of 1,800, beat a retreat.

Roberts could no longer be held from his main objective by such tactics, however exasperating. His whole force converged and Pretoria fell. Botha still held a strong position at Diamond Hill, east of Pretoria. Broadwood, his effectives reduced to 700, was sent to dislodge him, with orders to dash through a gap in the hills and occupy Eland's River Station in the enemy rear. The 10th Hussars got into effective action to the right, but the remainder of the brigade was held by heavy fire from the height of the Boer position.

The main threat was again to the guns and the 12th Lancers were sent into the charge, covered by the fire of the dismounted Household Cavalry. This danger overcome, Life Guards and Blues swung into the saddle and chased the enemy over mealie fields with the greatest zest. The main Boer position was occupied next day.

The hunt was now up and even guerilla fighters were of no avail against the mobile British columns which ranged the land for the next two years. It was estimated – perhaps too early – that there were now sufficient troops available for all likely purposes in South Africa and the Composite Regiment of Household Cavalry was recalled, arriving in England in November, 1900.

It took King Edward VII in person to straighten out an error in nomenclature of the lowest Household Cavalry rank. It is not clear when exactly the rank 'trooper' came into use – probably in 1788, certainly during the wars against Napoleon. The King was surprised – annoyed might be the better word – to find that the medals he handed out for the recent war were inscribed 'Private'. Authority ventured a mild protest when the medals – on royal orders – were handed back for re-engraving. The

The Cavalryman's creed starts with the sentence, 'The Horse comes first.' A trooper of the First Life Guards, dismounting from the King's Life Guard in 1908, waters his horse at Regents Park Barracks.
Photo by Mrs. Albert Broom, photographer to the Household Brigade

title was changed officially and borne by the Household Cavalry alone until after the First World War.

Chapter 10

The Great War

Two captains of the Second Life Guards slumped into corner seats of the train that was to take them from Windsor to Southampton and the 'Great War'. They had had a tiring morning, getting up far too early, inspecting soldiery, riding down to the station, loading baggage and fractious horses. Captain Adrian Bethell glanced across at Sir Archibald Sinclair.

'Well, Archie,' he sighed, 'we never thought it would come to this, did we?'

Perhaps it was just an early morning thought, for it hardly reflected the mood of nation or Army. Britain had been looking askance at Germany for long enough, at least as far back as 1871, when Prussia's victory over Napoleon III had destroyed the sacred 'balance of power' on which British foreign policy was based. Since then an expanding German economy, her development of colonies, the building of a High Seas Fleet and the occasional indiscretions of Kaiser Wilhelm were seen as tangible threats.

Now the German invasion of Belgium had but legalised what most Britons thought and almost wished. In the enemy camp thought was even clearer, summarised without compromise in the *Hamburger Nachrichten:* 'We have taken the field against Russia and France but at bottom it is England we are fighting everywhere. . . . It is from England we must wring the uttermost price for this gigantic struggle.'

With war declared, 'England' – since Germany insisted on the term – refused to worry about the future. There was a Russian 'steamroller' gathering way, a French army that, conscript and therefore suspect though it was, looked extremely gallant and delightfully old-fashioned in red trousers. On our own side of the Channel the Territorials had volunteered almost to a man for overseas service: men were besieging the recruiting offices. This surely was a waste of time and effort – it would be over by Christmas. Only from Whitehall came a sombre note, where Lord Kitchener, hastily appointed War Minister, entered his office for the first time.

'Dear me,' he exclaimed, 'What a War Office: no army: no staff and,' – flinging aside a War Department pen, 'not even a pen that will write.'

* * *

Details of the First Life Guards parade at Knightsbridge before leaving for the Great War of 1914-18.

Photo by Mrs. Albert Broom

Despite the fact that the Household Cavalry now had their own reserve, it was still essentially a long-service force. Men were prone to 'soldier on'. Corporals with less than four years' service were a rarity and made the step to corporal of horse with ten or twelve. South African medals were almost a badge among higher ranks and one officer – Quartermaster of the First Life Guards – rode to war with the decorations he had earned in Egypt in 1882. Consequently, the Household Cavalry at war could only consist of the now familiar Composite Regiment.

Under the mobilisation scheme it was commanded and staffed by whichever regiment was at Knightsbridge, now the First Life Guards, with Lieutenant-Colonel E. B. Cook, M.V.O., who was to be an early casualty, as Commanding Officer. The Regiment which, with the 6th Carabineers and the 3rd Hussars, made up the 4th Cavalry Brigade, had an old comrade as Brigadier. The Hon. C. E. Bingham had a unique career, having been Adjutant of the Second Life Guards and Commanding Officer of the First and was later to be full colonel of his original regiment. The Regiment embarked at Southampton on August 15, were over the Belgian frontier by the 21st and made immediate contact with German patrols. The Cavalry Division under Allenby consisted of four brigades, with a fifth acting independently.

Plan and command were French but it was the classical British opening to a war. The French advance into Alsace was purely political: the British, under protest, posted too far forward, regiments marching straight from railhead into their battle positions. Yet the B.E.F. had no cause for regret in its early skirmishes and was only dismayed that it was ordered to commence the 'Retreat from Mons'. Sir John French, its Commander-in-Chief, may not have been the easiest man for the Allies to work with, but he could justly complain that his left flank was constantly in the air by unannounced French retreat.

It was to the left that he deployed his cavalry and the 4th Cavalry Brigade was in action at Halte, Saultain (where they dug their first trenches), Compiégne and Néry, not realising that they narrowly missed being bottled up in Mauberge.

On September 3 the Regiment reached Lognes, ten miles from the outskirts of Paris, but the enemy had reached the limit of his advance. Von Klück had lost touch with the British he planned to destroy and Joffre turned to fight the decisive battles of Marne and Aisne, names on the Standards earned by sound work, both mounted and on foot. The campaign now swayed northwards and the B.E.F. was rushed by rail to what was, for it, the vital area covering the ports. That the Allies won the race was due, primarily, to the fact that the German high command had not obeyed Molkte's dictum: 'Let the right flank man brush the Channel with his cuff.'

The Composite Regiment saw its first action on the new front at Warneton where, on October 21, they lost both their Commanding Officer and the squadron leader of the First Life Guards, Lord John Cavendish. Fighting was fierce at Wytschaete on the night of October 31/November 1, with the enemy gaining a foothold in the First Life Guards trenches. They were driven out, leaving a plentiful bag of prisoners behind, but it was almost the last action of the Composite Regiment, as such.

* * *

Back home, a vast expansion of the Army was in progress and each regiment of Life Guards, with barracks bursting at the seams, formed its reserve regiment. They had material to spare and the country needed every man. In the cavalry depots were the reservists of line cavalry regiments in India, always kept at war strength. These, added to the cadres left behind when the Composite Regiment sailed, were sufficient to make up a whole cavalry Brigade, the Seventh, which was formed at Ludgershall. Line regiments from Egypt and South Africa completed the 3rd Cavalry Division which, with the 7th Division of infantry, was sent under Rawlinson on the abortive attempt to save Antwerp. The force landed at Zeebrugge and elsewhere on October 8. For the troops it was a repetition of the welcome which the 'Contemptibles' had received, until even the staid War Diary remarked: 'It seems undesirable for troops to remain halted in friendly towns.'

'Too little and too late' sealed the fate of Antwerp, but there was work and to spare in the open Belgian country. There was the obvious need for a link-up with the main allied forces. Rawlinson withdrew gradually until the ominous name of 'Ypres' appeared in an operation order for the first time, on October 13. Fighting was heavy and continuous: all thought of the 'cavalry role' was suspended. Only the rifle and the occasional machine gun counted, with the light screen of field guns behind.

The Life Guards saw heavy fighting on October 20 at Passchendaele, and were next deployed on Zandvoorde Ridge, a position of great importance opposite which the enemy was piling up like a tidal wave. On the morning of October 30 three much-weakened cavalry divisions were stretched along nine miles of a forward slope. In reserve were two Indian battalions: in support their own Horse Gunners and a section of six-inch howitzers. The German high command announced: 'We will finish with the British, Indians, Moroccans and other trash,' then, at 6.45 am, 260 pieces opened up on the cavalry. Just over an hour later an infantry division and three light battalions advanced up the ridge where the Seventh Cavalry Brigade lay in hastily-scooped trenches. The brigade order ran, from right to left: squadron First Life Guards, squadron Second Life Guards, Blues machine gunners, squadron First Life Guards, squadron Second Life Guards.

Retirement was inevitable and the majority came back quietly over the ridge through the sixth Brigade in reserve. But Lord Hugh Grosvenor's squadron of the First, Captain Vandeleur's of the Second and the Blues' machine gunners were extinguished almost entirely. It was a fitting spot for the Household Cavalry memorial, which stands there today.

On the morning of November 6 the Brigade, reduced to 600 men (400 if dismounted for action) stood-to in Sanctuary Wood at Hooge. They were in reserve to Cavan's 4th Guards Brigade, whose neighbours were a few elderly French territorials. At 2 pm the French, under continuous fire, started to trickle back. It was Germany's moment: if she succeeded now the Channel ports were hers. The First Irish Guards, minus one company which had literally been blown to pieces, formed a defensive flank until they could be reinforced by the First Life Guards. The Second Life Guards took the village of Zwartelen with the bayonet (which they had never been trained to use) and held the famous Hill Sixty position, losing in Major Hugh Dawnay, temporarily in command, one of the Army's most promising younger officers.

A confused night followed, during which the relief of the cavalry was commenced by a weak battalion of the Gloucestershire Regiment. The story is rounded off by the adventures of the 2nd Life Guards' adjutant who wandered off and got lost in the dark. His attempt at speaking French to a German outpost was not a success, but he made his way to safety by singing 'God save the King' to the astonished Gloucesters!

The whole affair has been described as a 'dog fight', and an example of determined men being hurled into a combat between tired troops at a critical moment. The Commander-in-Chief thought it 'doubtful whether the annals of the British Army contain any record finer than this,' while the King himself declared, 'It was the masterly way in which you were led by Generals Byng and Kavanagh (divisional and brigade commanders) that enabled us to hold and maintain the position we occupy today.' Ypres and the Channel ports were saved.

The losses of the Household Cavalry could only be replaced from one immediate source. The Composite Regiment itself had suffered heavy losses; it was now broken up and, on November 11, 1914, was ordered to disperse, every man to his own regiment. In the First Life Guards the ex-composite squadron became 'B' and remained, throughout the war, representative of the original peace-time regiment, still riding the long-maned 'black 'uns' who plodded along the wretched roads of Flanders as equably as the processional streets of London. The letter 'C' was left blank in tribute to the gallant squadron which lay forever along the Zandvoorde Ridge. The Blues left the Seventh Cavalry Brigade, being replaced by the Leicestershire Yeomanry, one of several yeomanry regiments sent out at this time.

* * *

There was more to war than plain fighting, battles against others than the Germans took place. Veterans may still remember the 'Plum and Apple Scandal', highlighted by Bruce Bairnsfather's cartoon of an old soldier opening a tin of jam and asking: 'When the 'ell is it going to be strawberry?' The War Office took action in a reassuring letter of February 15, 1915, also recorded in the War Diary.

> 'PLUM AND APPLE JAM. We are now sending other kinds of jam and some marmalade. . . . I would suggest that base depots be told to issue anything in the way of jam they have except plum and apple. . . . At the end of a month or two, when the troops are tired of eating marmalade, they will probably greet the plum and apple as an old and welcome friend.' Alas, they never did.

Regiments took their turn in the dismal trench warfare which now developed, selected Territorial formations and more Indian troops giving them some relief. The opening battle of 1915 at Neuve Chapelle was a grievous dis-

Horse lines in front of Arras, April 1917. A Household Cavalry officer, much later, remarked: 'The horse has no place in modern war.'
Imperial War Museum

appointment. Although more ammunition for the guns had been piled than had been fired during the whole Boer War, it sufficed for a mere three days at Neuve Chapelle, after which the whole battle petered out.

It was now the turn of the enemy, who estimated rightly that Ypres was still the key. The evening of May 12 found the Seventh Cavalry Brigade holding the right centre of two cavalry divisions on the Ypres front. The First Life Guards were particularly vulnerable, the Bays on their right being 150 yards to the rear, while there was an ugly gap between their own two front-line squadrons. The B.E.F. was stretched to its utmost, paying for the neglect of its masters.

Three hours of concentrated enemy gunfire preceded a massive infantry attack in the small hours of the 13th. The line snapped and the Sixth and Seventh Brigades were forced to retire, except for one squadron of the First Life Guards who joined the Bays and a tiny detachment which clung to a small mound all day. By nightfall the position was restored, but the division had lost ninety-one officers and 1,052 men.

The so-called 'war of attrition' now set in, with the initiative usually, if fruitlessly, with the Allies. For the cavalry it meant years of frustrated hopes, with periods in the line as infantry and even more tedious stretches of trench digging. The Life Guards provided divisional cavalry for the Guards Division from their reserves in England and a Household Battalion was formed from the reserve regiments on September 1, 1916, and sent to join the 4th Division in France.

His Majesty struck the true note in his farewell message to the Battalion:

> 'This is the first occasion that an infantry battalion has been formed from the regiments of Household Cavalry. Remember that you are members of either the First Life Guards, second Life Guards or Blues and I am convinced that as infantry you will maintain the splendid traditions which are the pride of these regiments.'

The Household Battalion was true to its Colonel-in-Chief and its parent regiments, but heavy casualties and man-power difficulties dictated its disbandment in January, 1918. It had added its chapter to the history of its regiments and its passing was resented by the generals under whose command it had served. The divisional commander wrote of one occasion: 'This feat of skill and endurance in the mud of Flanders (this in October, 1917) was a fitting climax to your former deeds.'

In the face of all the evidence, the command clung to the belief that horsed cavalry would still prove an effective weapon until, in the early days of 1918, it was forced to admit that five mounted divisions was more than it would ever be likely to need. Indian regiments were sent to a more suitable theatre, most of the Yeomanry were dis-mounted, while Life Guards and Blues were converted to a new role. They were turned into lorry-borne machine gunners, trained on special lines to form a G.H.Q. reserve which could be plugged into the line.

Regret at parting with the horses was modified by the thought that they, at any rate, would be saved further suffering. Anxiety was felt for the status and prestige of the regiments but these were safeguarded. They retained titles, badges and pay and even the redundant farriers still wore horseshoes on their jackets. There was a pleasant training interlude on the sands outside Etaples, marred by a vicious air raid on the night of Whit Sunday, which cost the First Life Guards' forty-three killed and eighty-two wounded and introduced them to a new, even more hateful form of warfare.

The new job was a challenge to men who had been frustrated for so long. A whole machine gun school was brought out from England to train them. The regiments, as now constituted, could concentrate all their zeal on the task: they did not even have to drive the vehicles in which they rode, the internal combustion engine being the strict preserve of the Army Service Corps.

The First Life Guards were first committed near Arras, the second at Warlay, as the army waited for the follow-up to the enemy's spring offensive. The First Life Guards manned one of the 'switch lines' into which the German advance was to be diverted and local operations included an attack across the Scarpe with the 51st Highland Division. The Seconds were employed around Albert and took part in the breaching of the formidable Hindenburg Line. The great attraction of the new battalions was that they were capable of taking on tasks beyond the scope of normal machine gun battalions. They were not so popular with the ordinary infantryman, when their 'hit and run' tactics brought down enemy retaliation – the real culprits being safe and far away.

The Household Cavalry were the main ingredient of

what was Britain's first mechanised force. Mobility was once more a word to conjure with. Two of the three battalions, each of sixty-four machine guns, were joined by a lorried Guards brigade, with a battery of guns run up into lorries, plus a hapless battalion of men on push bikes. Such a force covered the advance to St. Quentin which rid a whole section of France from the invaders.

War was now a long-distance affair, but it was given to two gun teams of the Second Life Guards to see the frightened whites of their enemies' eyes. Lieutenant Gunther an his men had spent a wretched week in a ruined cellar at Sequehart, strafed day and night, when they were warned to give covering fire to two attacks, one British and the other French, to either side of them. The British, in the form of a battalion of the Monmouths – were practically

Machine gunners of the First Life Guards heading for St. Quentin late in 1918.

Courtesy the Daily Mirror

destroyed: the French did little better, being tied down by machine gun fire.

At last the look-out on the battered chimney called down: 'I can see 'em; come up and have a look,' and there, almost out of range, were their opposite numbers. There was a crest beyond a stretch of open ground. If they could reach it it would give them a fire position. They crawled up to it and then, after three ranging bursts, saw their foes on the run. Then, even as they relaxed, came a 'tornado of fire swishing and crackling like all the devils in hell.' It developed into a private duel until the French, in a last effort, cleared the front. Finally, eighty yards away, the teams of ten enemy guns, ragged and shaken, rose to their feet and surrendered to the Life Guards. It was, they felt, worth waiting a whole war for.

The whole urge was now forward and the Armistice

Men of the Life Guards, invalided home or wounded, were presented with the 'Mons Star' on Horse Guards Parade early in 1918, first of the Army to receive it.

Photo by Mrs. Albert Broom

found both regiments on the Belgian frontier, keyed up for the offensive which never came. News of the Armistice was received with the stoicism of the regular soldier, to whom this war was an episode, not a complete story. In the First Regiment it was celebrated by hot baths in Lille. By March, 1919 they were home in Knightsbridge and Windsor.

Since 1914 the three regiments of Household Cavalry had provided a composite regiment, a cavalry brigade, a divisional squadron and a cyclist company, the Household Battalion and a Household Siege Battery. Serving soldiers, reservists, men re-enlisted, soldiers of the line and 'duration' men, all found a common bond and inspiration in the regimental system which has been the basis of the British Army.

Chapter II

The Second World War

RARELY has the Army been subjected to such a series of blows as those rained upon it from 1919 onwards – those which were to come in the second half of the century being mercifully veiled from its eyes. There had been no general reduction of the army since Waterloo. Now, with the 'war to end all wars' fought to nominal victory, the nation saddled with debt largely contracted to help others out, and with the promise of a 'land fit for heroes to live in', the army was fair game. The cavalry, in particular, was seen as thirty-one expensive regiments which had collected few headlines since 1914.

Public outcry against the disbandment of the four junior line cavalry regiments led to a last-minute substitution of amalgamation and the practice was extended to reduce the twenty-eight line regiments to twenty, two of them, the 11th Hussars and the 12th Lancers, being converted to armoured cars. The 'Geddes Axe' (as the system was called from its sponsor) descended also upon the Life Guards, the two regiments being reduced to one in 1922 and stationed first at Regent's Park, which was considered the final indignity.

The Regiment was first known as 'The Life Guards (First and Second)' later simplified into 'The Life Guards' when it was realised that the change must be permanent. The whole process looked simple from the outside but within barracks there was almost an armed neutrality. The old regiments were fiercely individualistic, the First Life Guards being apt to refer to themselves as 'The First Regiment' while their comrades were apt to mutter 'Nulli Secundus' – as they had probably done since 1788!

The Guards, in March 1919, were the first troops to be awarded a 'Victory March' through London. The First Life Guards head the procession down Fleet Street.

On the practical side there were fourteen differences in uniform and equipment: even the scarlet stripes on the overalls being of different widths. Most noticeable were the sheepskins over the saddles, being black for the First Regiment and white for the Second. White being historically correct, it was adopted for the whole Regiment, except in the band. In the long run the whole problem of amalgamation was solved by sheer goodwill and plain commonsense. The Army had other things to worry about than the colour of a pouchbelt cord or on which side of its neck a horse's mane should be trained.

One difference remained. When, in June 1925, His Majesty presented new Standards, the Life Guards received two Sovereign's Standards and four squadron, still with the slight difference in Battle Honours granted for the last war. But these were the last Standards granted to the old regiments as such. The Household Cavalry are the only regiments to continue the historic practice of squadron Standards. While all of them carry the full list of Battle Honours, the Sovereign's Standard bears the Royal Arms, the squadron Standards the 'Union' device of Rose, Thistle and Shamrock.

Regent's Park Barracks remained the 'town house' of the

In 1925 King George V presented new Standards to the Household Cavalry on Horse Guards Parade.

Regiment until 1932, when King George V took a hand. When, on an August Sunday, the Life Guards marched into Knightsbridge from manoeuvres there lay on the orderly room table a telegram from their Colonel-in-Chief, welcoming his Life Guards back to 'their old home'.

That the British Army is normally unprepared for war is not its own fault but that of the nation that has to pay for it. Taxpayers and their elected representatives for long sang themselves to sleep with the refrain, 'There will be no major war for ten years', but when it was realised that Mr. Chamberlain's tragic 'Peace in our time' was a myth, the nation awoke. It had overslept its alarm clock. The Army, if it was fit for anything, was only designed to dig itself once more into the mud of Flanders.

Feverish last-minute attempts at mechanisation were far too feeble for the 'Panzer' divisions which lurked over the Rhine. We entered the war with two armoured car regiments (one of them in Egypt), the few battalions of the Royal Tank Corps and a wreck of untrained, unequipped ex-cavalry regiments. The Household Cavalry, Royals, Scots Greys and a few of the Yeomanry were still horsed. It is popular to blame out-dated generals with a vested interest in the horse, but most of them were dead and all retired, while within the regiments were a majority with minds modern enough to see into the near future.

War found Life Guards and Blues with a mobilisation scheme ten years old. It provided for a regiment allotted to the 1st (and only) Cavalry Division, a Training Regiment at Windsor and a Reserve Regiment in London. The new composite regiment was commanded and staffed by the Life Guards, a practice which continued. The fact that a second regiment was formed under Blues' command made it easy (but incorrect) to regard the first and second regiments as Life Guards and Blues respectively. But in point of fact these were for the first time really 'composite', even within squadrons.

It is not the intention here to attempt anything like a war history of the Life Guards. The canvas is far too broad and a general sketch has already been given in another book of this series.*

The Composite Regiment was shipped to Palestine

In 1939 the King's Life Guard did duty at Whitehall, dismounted and in service dress. Later the Guard was withdrawn after the buildings were bombed.

early in 1940 with Europe preparing to go up in flames behind it. The faithful 'long-faced pals' went too, and the 1st Cavalry Division stood complete, but with its regiments already looking forward to a role within the framework of modern war. The Household Cavalry had had a taste of forcible conversion in 1918 and now staked their claim on the armoured car, for which they saw themselves as ideal material. Events proved them right, but it was to be a long

* *The Royal Horse Guards* in the Famous Regiment Series, by R. J. T. Hills.

and boring way from the saddle to the driving wheel or gun.

To regular soldiers a move was a move, whether from London to Windsor or to the Middle East. There must be an 'advance party', so that two officers, the regimental quartermaster corporal and two reservists (with one prehistoric typewriter) climbed into a truck and thence travelled by various methods to Haifa, where the weather seemed perilously like that which they thought they had left behind. But at Tulkarm they found civilised soldiering again – plus orange blossom and Arab sanitation.

The Regiment followed: the horses got over their first terror of the camel: and the men topped up with sun helmets, with red and blue piping to their bands.

Oddly enough it was the regiments in England that were first declared to be 'on active service', with the Reserve Regiment in Knightsbridge seeing the distinct possibility of adding 'LONDON – 1940' to the Battle Honours! It was a steady regiment, made up of reservists, the Band of the Life Guards, sixty aged horses, one furniture van and a decrepit motor-cycle, reinforced by six motor coaches whose drivers only worked union hours. It made barricades for the Park by wrapping barbed wire round the riding-school jumps, made its own Molotov cocktails and reconnoitred a battle position known as 'The Acton Line'. The King's Life Guard was maintained in Whitehall, dismounted and in service dress.

The Training Regiment at Windsor was expanded, slowly gave up the pretence of being horsed cavalry until, late in 1941, it was able to move to Bulford as the 'Household Cavalry Motor Regiment', later the 'Second Household Cavalry Armoured Car Regiment', and finally, when the Army had got used to it, as '2HCR'.

The history of the Regiment in Palestine was at first overshadowed by the difficulties of re-equipment, with Britain at her last gasp for warlike stores. Dogged persistence and improvisation got it fit and at least lorry-borne for

Italian prisoners being brought into the POW compounds in North Africa in 1942, escorted by armoured cars of the Household Cavalry.

the occupation of Baghdad and Teheran, with the brisk dash and neat action at the Palmyra Oasis when it became necessary to deal with the Vichy French in Syria.

The first of these actions was made necessary by the siege of the R.A.F. base at Habbaniya and the threat to the oil pipeline, and was undertaken by the *ad hoc* 'Habforce'. The Quartermaster, who in war or peace reckoned with a brick office, a wooden hut or at least a tent in the shade, had his own recollections of the advance in temperatures of up to 120 degrees F., with dirty rationed water, rendering life almost insupportable to spick and span soldiers.

The Quartermaster had the only new vehicle in the column, a Chrysler Plymouth, but wished for something less conspicuous when a mass of bright red 'marbles' bouncing in the road proved to be a welcome from an Iraqi biplane. Action over, they settled down at Habbaniya with green lawns, bottled Guinness – and a signpost giving the mileage to London. They were even congratulated on their freedom from sandfly – the Quartermaster having forgotten to hand in the nets in Palestine.

Distances came to mean little to the men of the new regiment. They had their first look at Cyprus, penetrated to the Turkish frontier and took their place in Montgomery's Eighth Army. Desert war makes exciting reading in today's armchair but included its periods of sheer boredom, mitigated by long-range purchases in Alexandria. These included twenty-four alarm clocks which a commanding officer, objecting to the normal practice of sounding reveille by firing a Bren gun, issued to every troop leader.

The final stage in the long march was to Italy, where the Regiment landed on April 12, 1943. Despite the long fight up the leg of Italy, it was regarded as a 'wonderful' interlude, though the weather often gave the lie to the pamphlets of the tourist agencies. There is a picture of a descendant of the cavalry commander at Waterloo awaking in a leaky tent on the morning after landing in Italy, his underclothing awash under his camp bed and the local women pawing over the dustbins outside.

Although there was enough fighting still ahead in Italy, the capture of Rome had in fact set the seal on the campaign, while the mighty sweep of Allied victory to the north made the end certain, however long it might be delayed. In addition, most of the personnel were due for home service, including nearly all its senior ranks, both commissioned and non-commissioned. Consequently the Regiment sailed from Naples as a whole for England on October 10, 1944.

Despite home ties and leave the men sometimes regretted they were, for a space, no longer at war, which they understood, instead of on home service, which bored them. Their immediate fate was Aldershot, where they occupied that mausoleum of Victorian cavalry, Beaumont Barracks, – 'out of date, damp and in deplorable repair'. It was an added reproach that while they, the veterans, suffered a Hampshire winter, their 'juniors' were gathering laurels under Montgomery.

The Second Household Cavalry Regiment was no longer the experimental unit that had been born at Windsor. Its mechanisation had been difficult enough but had gone faster and easier than that of the senior partner. To such an extent had it learned its job that when the great invasion opened it could lay just claim to the title of the most efficient armoured car regiment available for the decisive battle. The most exacting generals were glad to see it Earmarked at first for service with VIII Corps, the Regiment landed in France on July 13, in time for the break-out which swept the German armies over the Seine.

The story of the Regiment in North-west Europe reads like romantic drama. It was romance in its exciting, almost non-stop race over the battlefields: drama in its toll of gallant young gentlemen fighting their country's greatest battle. In its comparatively short campaign the Regiment had nearly eighty killed, 140 wounded and thirty taken prisoner.

Their earliest notable exploit, while under O'Connor's VIII Corps, was the brilliant seizure of the bridge over the Souleuvre in June by a lone half troop. So important was this feat, quickly followed up, that the whole plan of battle was changed to take advantage of it. It has even been described as the turning-point of the campaign in Normandy – a high estimate not made from within the Regiment itself. To the army the bridge was henceforth known as 'Cavalry Bridge'.

They were not to remain under their original corps, but their corps commander for the major part of the campaign has left no doubt as to his own estimate of their worth. O'Conner's description of some of their exploits cannot be bettered.

> 'It is probable,' he wrote, 'that the battle honours most prized in the Regiment are *Faith, Hope and Charity*, the code names given to the three Somme bridges which they

captured so successfully on August 31, 1944. . . . It was imperative to take every possible risk to seize the bridges before the Germans had time to organise their defence. The orders to advance were only received at 0100 hours and the ensuing advance must have been a nightmare; the men were already tired before they started, it was pouring with rain, and the roads were blocked by every form of traffic, including German tanks. Nevertheless, the leading troops pushed on relentlessly and the seemingly impossible was achieved – the bridges were all captured intact. But, what was even more important, having enlisted and armed members of the French Resistance, the Regiment held these bridges for four hours until the Grenadiers arrived – a most memorable night's work which could only have been achieved by well-trained, determined men whose morale was high.'

He quotes another 'striring example of the same sort, the capture of a vital bridge at Louvain by Lieutenant Hanbury's Troop. Corporal of Horse Thompson gave a remarkable exhibition of initiative and bravery when he found an alternative way across the Dyle, although this entailed getting out of the car and bridging the gap in the road with broken-down doors under intense small-arms fire.' For this exploit he was awarded the D.C.M.

Patrol warfare was merely an incident in 'Tommy's' life. He had been a riding instructor in 1939 and reverted to type when Hitler was finished. He won the King's Cup and was second in the Prince of Wales Cup at Olympia in 1949 and in the year following was first, second and third in the King's Cup, first and second in the Prince of Wales Cup. In 1951 he was commissioned as Riding Master, sole representative of an almost forgotten trade in the British Army.

The Regiment worked for various masters – that was part of its trade as an armoured car regiment. But they were happiest in the Guards Armoured Division – who referred to them as 'The Stable Boys'. They spoke the same language, shared the same jokes – became slightly pompous when 'outsiders' tried to butt in. Perhaps the somewhat ponderous habits of thought in the Guards Armoured was enlivened by their efforts to keep pace with the nimble riders who led the way; for the cavalrymen it was a reversion to the happiest form. Some of the battlefields were familiar to their regimental ancestors, but they were too busy making history to read it.

Constantly employed, never failing, the armoured cars hurtled through the war. But the highlight, the operation which restored, if only for a day, the old glamour, was the liberation of Brussels in September, with Life Guards and Blues in the van of the Guards' tumultuous advance.

This was almost a private war, in the Guards' own style, precise as a 'Trooping' on Horse Guards Parade, with the confidence that, as in London, nothing could go wrong. As dark was falling on a cold September 2, Major-General Adair held a conference on the outskirts of Douai.

'My intention,' he said, 'is to advance and liberate Brussels,' adding 'That is a grand intention'. It was, in fact, a jaunt of ninety miles, but the Guards did just what he intended.

There is no space to record the adventures of that glad day except to record that the 'first in' were two Household Cavalrymen in a scout car – Lance Corporal of Horse I. W. Dewar of Aberdeen and Trooper D. Ayles of London. The streets were deserted until Dewar brought out a small Union Jack. This did the trick.

'The Belgians,' said Dewar, 'made one mighty rush at us and we were completely swamped. I tried to get a message over but the aerials had already been whipped off as souvenirs. So had our bedding, all our rations, the cooker and everything else.' Only determined action by the police saved the wheels!

Small wonder that among its proudest trophies the Household Cavalry values among the highest the Brussels Standard it received from the Burgomaster in July of the

The Burgomaster of Brussels, Monsieur M. J. van de Meulebroeck, presents a Standard to the Second Household Cavalry Regiment, July 1945.
Photograph in possession of a member of the Regiment. Reproduced by kind permission of Major R. P. G. Orde, from his history of the Regiment.

following year.

The advance into Holland to link up with Browning's Airborne Forces was high adventure which ended in the tragedy of the 1st British Airborne Division at Arnhem. But the Household Cavalry had just cause to be proud of their share in this battle, fought 'on the width of one road'. Their ultimate object, the relief of 1st Airborne, failed but they made three vital link-ups in the general scheme – with the 82nd U.S. Airborne Division at Eindhoven, with the 101st U.S. Airborne at Grave and with the Polish Brigade at Driel.

There was one lifeguardsman at General Browning's Airborne Headquarters. He can guarantee that the finest sight of his soldiering was that of the armoured car that passed him just outside Nijmegen, with a lean and nonchalant trooper of his own Regiment towering from its turret.

Despite the check in Holland the end – though not quite in sight – was round the corner. Even von Runstedt's final thrust in the Ardennes, useless as it turned out to be, gave trouble which could have been more easily met. U.S. Intelligence discounted warnings from Montgomery's experts and part of the German thrust was met by raw troops thinly disposed and weakly backed up. In the holding movement carried out under Montgomery's command the Regiment played its due part and went on to the triumphant breaching of the Rhine barrier.

The First Regiment, refreshed and re-equipped, were in at the death, coming from England so that, when the 'Cease Fire' sounded, the full force of His Majesty's Household Cavalry was deployed for battle on enemy soil.

Chapter 12

The Age of Brinkmanship

THIS time the cessation of hostilities brought no getting back to 'real soldiering'. Beyond the Atlantic a politician invented the word 'brinkmanship' which allowed him and his like to glower at one another while, if anyone got hurt, it was merely a few soldiers or obscure villagers. In warlike or 'policing' events up and down the world the Life Guards have played their full share, anywhere between Hong Kong and Ulster.

It was an uncanny world into which the Regiment was reborn. A slip-up in map-reading could land the unwary in the midst of querulous Russians or, in one case, of a fully-armed German army marching to demobilisation – 'field-grey marching masses stretching to the horizon'. Fortunately, reflected the officer concerned, they seemed totally unaffected by defeat, singing themselves out of history with their traditional automatic rhythm.

On September 1, 1945 the two Household Cavalry Regiments shook themselves out to become once again the Life Guards and Royal Horse Guards (the Blues). With both regiments close at hand it was a fairly simple matter and even the Quartermaster admitted 'it did not seem too difficult at the time. It was odd,' he continued, 'for a week or two having so many strange faces around, but adjustment was soon made to the everyday routine.' In other words the regiments were able to continue their steady history of nearly three hundred years. Wartime comradeship had been precious, but the old identities were fundamental.

First peace-time station of the Regiment was Wölfenbüttel, where the old ceremony of 'Hanging the Brick' in the

The W.O.s and N.C.O.s mark the opening of the Christmas season by 'Hanging the Brick'. The Brick-hanger of 1923 was still the donor of the Brick, Mr. Joe Holland, for many years Forage Master of the Second Life Guards.

warrant and non-commissioned officers' mess as a signal of Christmas festivities was resumed. There are several legends as to the origin of the ceremony but in any case it is well over a hundred years old, having been taken over in 1922 from the Second Life Guards as part of the amalgamation. The brick used is a special one kept in an ebony and silver casket and presented long ago by Mr. Joe Holland, civilian forage master of the Second Life Guards. It remains hung over the bar from Christmas Eve until New Year's Day. Mr. Holland himself hung the brick until his death and it has since been hung by a retired regimental corporal major, or, if distance prevents, by the commanding officer.

After a quick shake-down, the Regiment moved into

shattered Berlin, living in something like luxury out by the Wannsee, with a brief period in Lüneburg. Berlin life was hectic, if worrying for commanding officers, with the black market in full swing and troops letting their pay credits pile up while they lived well enough by selling their surplus cigarettes and chocolate. There was only passing reference to training and leave was plentiful, it being commonplace to take a seat in a Dakota at 10.30 am and have tea in London. But it did not last long.

In July 1946, the Life Guards moved back to the Middle East, divided at first between Cairo and Alexandria, then re-united at Fanara in the Canal Zone. The old soldiers were unmoved by the romance of the 'Shiny East'. For them it was 'the same arid heat like the blast from a furnace, the stinking latrines and the countless millions of Egyptian house-flies, the same braying donkey – and the same gippy tummy'. The same standards of pilfering still ruled. A storeman sleeping alongside a large crate of instruments did not prevent a small boy creeping in with a rope attached to a camel and making off with an assortment of binoculars, compasses and watches. One reliable N.C.O., travelling in a non-stop jeep to Cairo, arrived minus his Sten gun.

Egypt was followed by a year of trouble-shooting in Palestine, arising out of the U.N. decision to partition the country, with British troops standing between Jewish and Arab irregular forces. In August 1948, the Life Guards sailed for home from Port Said and saw Windsor for the first time since the troubles had started.

Meanwhile a peace time pattern of life had been worked out for the Household Cavalry as a whole. The horse having been eliminated from war, it was necessary only to maintain the minimum of mounted men for state duties. Consequently a new mounted regiment with a squadron from each regiment was formed at Knightsbridge, while the two armoured car regiments (the Life Guards and Royal Horse Guards [the Blues]) relieved each other for training at Windsor or duty abroad. To command the whole a 'regimental lieutenant-colonel' with a small staff had been set up during the war years, so conforming with the long practice of the Foot Guards. To confound the outsider, the 'lieutenant-colonel' is a full colonel and carries out the function of Silverstick.

After three and a half years of home service the Regiment returned to Germany in March, 1952 – a short stay broken by a strong detachment taking part in the Coronation and receiving new Standards at the hands of Her Majesty. The whole Regiment was home by November of 1953 but only to prepare for another leap back to the Canal Zone, where there was mounting opposition to the presence of British troops.

An armoured car regiment is particularly adapted for internal security duties, each of its squadrons and even troops being capable of acting as an independent unit. There were two deployments of this nature in 1955, detachments being made to Aden and Cyprus. 'Trouble Island' was now in the grip of the EOKA terror and a troop was sent as an escort for the Governor-General, later Field-Marshal Sir John Harding and Colonel of the Regiment. This was increased to a squadron, detailed to escort vital convoys.

Time was running out in Egypt and when the Regiment came home, in March 1956, it left one squadron in the Canal Zone. These men, with the 2nd Grenadier Guards, were the last troops to leave Egypt, which they had first seen in 1882. The Regiment was now given a new role – that of a regiment of the Strategic Reserve to be carried by air, a highly mobile force capable of being sent to any trouble spot at short notice. Even the comfort of Windsor was comparative, the old barracks being in process of rebuilding, described by a commentator as the 'death of a thousand pickaxes'.

Rigid censorship prevented much news on the minor

Field-Marshal Lord Harding, Colonel of the Regiment, takes the salute of mounted and armoured squadrons in Windsor Great Park, 1958.

Courtesy of 'Soldier Magazine'

war in Arabia reaching the public, but the Life Guards saw enough of it and considered it far from 'minor'. Going to Aden in 1958, they were set for more than a year to hunt rebels in one of the hottest climates and some of the worst country in the world. In temperatures well over the hundred mark, the Ferret scout cars chased guerillas from tip to tip of the Southern Arabian peninsula.

Fortunately, it was hardly possible to transfer the Regiment from torrid Arabia to frostbound Germany without a call in England. But they were in Herford by January, 1959 and took up the 'cold war' task of patrolling the Iron Curtain, keeping a wary eye on the sullen communist troops over the way. It was a comparatively short stay before another return to the still squalid wastes of Windsor. The Regiment almost welcomed the order in 1964 to return to Cyprus, 'C' Squadron being airborne within forty-eight hours from the 'off'. The Regiment, or detach-

'C' Squadron The Life Guards, part of the British contingent of the U.N. Force, on convoy in Cyprus.

ments of it, were on the island until November, uncomfortable between armed bodies of Turks and Greeks, all with fingers itching.

In the following year both the Life Guards and Blues were honoured with the Freedom of the Royal Borough of Windsor, a distinction accepted with pride from the people of the town they had known since the reign of their founder. But next year the Regiment made its furthest spring – to Malaysia, a geographical term which proved merely approximate, since it included Singapore, Borneo and Hong Kong. It had been necessary to bring the Regiment up to strength with a squadron of the Blues, but these were gradually replaced, and the Life Guards themselves came home in October, 1968, to a Combermere Barracks no longer recognisable by old soldiers, even the front and back doors having changed places and with the 'Lord Raglan' no longer the nearest pub.

With the Army at its lowest ebb even a 'home service'

Freemen of the Royal Borough of Windsor. In 1965 both Regiments of Household Cavalry were honoured with the Freedom of Windsor. Bands and detachments in the picture march past the Guildhall on taking up their new privileges.

Courtesy of the Windor, Slough and Eton Express

regiment is allowed little rest and its very training programme entails frequent moves to other countries with other climates. Thus, in 1969, detachments were found in such varied spots as Norway, Denmark and Germany, subsequently arguing it out as to who had had the worst weather. Luckiest was the half squadron which was awarded a Mediterranean cruise on H.M.S. *Fearless*, with calls at Gibraltar and Sardinia.

Since the days of William III the Regiment had never considered Ireland as a battleground until, in mid-August of 1969, 'B' Squadron was put on forty-eight hours' notice for Ulster. Shanklin Road and 'No Go Land' became familiar to the armoured car crews, but three and a half months of what was perilously like civil war were more than enough. The troubles were damped down but by no means extinguished – in 1970 first one then two squadrons, with Regimental Headquarters, took part in this most distasteful form of military activity.

In 1969 and 1970 the Life Guards took their share of unpleasant duty in Northern Ireland. An armoured car heads a convoy in Belfast.

Meanwhile 'A' Squadron did a nine-months' 'unaccompanied' tour in Shahyah in the Persian Gulf and the Regiment provided a good example of what constitutes 'home service' in the new British Army. Finally, the Regiment is scheduled, during 1971, to be converted to Chieftain tanks and to be posted to Germany.

* * *

'It's all in the day's work,' is said to have been the dying remark of a private soldier of the regiment commanded by the youthful Arthur Wellesley. He was, according to tradition, Private Thomas Atkins, whose name was much later selected by the old Duke of Wellington to be filled in as typical on a new set of army forms.

The old soldier's words have become the slogan of the British Army. The Life Guards, formed as the personal bodyguard of King Charles II, continuing the same proud

There is little pomp and circumstance in modern Berlin. The Mounted Band of The Life Guards paraded in front of the Brandenburg Gate in 1969.

duty under his successors, have been committed to most duties for which the soldier may be called upon. With Britain at peace and the Army reduced to its very bones, the work is more varied than ever before. The soldier of the Seventies, refusing even to be surprised at the next order he receives, can only mutter through closed lips the old tag: 'Soldier on'.

The Life Guards Regimental March

THE Regimental March of the Life Guards, i.e. the Slow March, is a combination of those of the two regiments which amalgamated in 1922. That of the First Life Guards, reproduced here, was composed traditionally by H.R.H. the Duchess of Kent, mother of Queen Victoria, especially for the Regiment. The March of the Second Life Guards, both in slow and quick time, was 'Men of Harlech'. This remains officially as part of the Regimental March but is rarely used owing to the undue length of the combined marches. It is not printed here.

As a Regimental Quick March, 'Milanollo', shared with the Coldstream Guards, was for long the Quick March of the First Life Guards and is used when the Regiment parades on foot.

1st
2nd
p
f
1st
2nd